BR STEAM MOTIVE POWER DEPOTS

BR STEAM MOTIVE POWER DEPOTS

ER

Paul Bolger

Nottingham

Booklaw Publications

First published 1982

© Ian Allan 1982

This edition published by
Book Law Publications 2009

Printed and Bound by
The Amadeus Press, Cleckheaton, BD19 4TQ.

Preface

The purpose of this book is to assist the average enthusiast be he modeller, relic collector or historian, with his search for information on Motive Power Depots — the home of the steam locomotive.

Many devotees will recall the experience of touring such an establishment; the hiss of steam, the clank of engine movements and the sight of smoke suspended from the ceilings above the many varieties of engine in different stages of repair.

The sight of a fully serviced locomotive simmering outside the Depot on a crisp bright morning is a memory I shall never forget. I hope that the following pages aid the reminiscences of those fortunate enough to have lived during the steam age.

This book is dedicated to my father, Charles Bolger, who died suddenly prior to the publication of the LMR volume. His active interest is sadly missed.

Paul Bolger

Introduction

For reasons of parity with the previous volume — *BR Steam Motive Power Depots LMR* (Ian Allan) — the depots covered by this work have been restricted to those which possessed a code, as these were the most visited and of greater importance to the railway network.

In all, 50 depots are outlined and because of the lesser number of sheds by comparison with the LMR volume, two views per shed have been included for all but three venues. For continuity of the text the codes used as headings are, in the majority, c1950.

Acknowledgements

This book has been made possible with the invaluable help of the following people and organisations: Mr G. Goslin of the Gresley Society; Mr G. M. Kitchenside of Locomotive & General Railway Photographs; Mr Rhodes of Real Photographs; Mr C. Turner of Photomatic; Miss S. Percy of the Ordnance Survey.

Special thanks are due to the following for their assistance with the photographs and plans: H. I. Cameron; W. A. Camwell; H. C. Casserley; R. Clow; F. Dean; A. G. Ellis; K. Fairey; C. I. K. Field; V. Forster; B. K. B. Green; L. Hanson; B. Hilton; M. S. Houlgrave; G. Jones; P. J. Kelley; F. Lyon; P. G. Martin; G. Maslin; W. Potter; N. E. Preedy; G. Reeve; D. Rendell; W. Stubbs; T. Wright; B. Yale; the staff of the British Museum Map Library.

In the course of preparation the following publications were of major importance as reference and consultative material: *The Railway Observer* (Volumes 20-38); *The Railway Magazine* (Volumes 94-114); *Railway World* (Volumes 19-29); *Trains Illustrated* and *Modern Railways* (Volumes 3 to 21).

Notes About Contents

The following ex-Midland Railway depots which moved to the Eastern Region from the London Midland Region have been catered for in the latter volume: (LMR codes in brackets) 35C Peterborough Spital Bridge (16B); 41B Sheffield Grimesthorpe (19A); 41C Millhouses (19B); 41D Canklow (19C); 41E Staveley Midland (18D).

The ex-LTS group of depots, 33A Plaistow, 33B Tilbury and 33C Shoeburyness have been included here as they became Eastern Region property soon after nationalisation and their exclusion would have created a numerical void within this volume.

Whilst is seems contradictory to exlude 35C for one reason and to include the 33 group for another, it must be remembered that strict compliance with the coding system would have resulted in severe duplication of the contents of this and the LMR volume. A balance has, therefore, been struck in an attempt to combat the effects of BR's failure to issue each region with its codes in January 1948. It is hoped that the resulting regional 'limbo' where it occurs will not hinder your enjoyment of the book.

Pre-Grouping Origins

Although, primarily, not relevant to the period covered, an indication of the vintage of the shed is given by the inclusion of the company of ownership prior to 1923. This is not necessarily the company which commissioned the building as many smaller installations were absorbed into the larger companies by the takeover or amalgamation of district railways.

Gazetteer References

These numbers refer to the page and square within the Ian Allan Pre-Grouping Atlas which pinpoint the subject's national location.

Closing Dates

The dates given indicate the closure of the depot to steam engines only. However, in some cases the date would have been the same for diesels where the building closed completely, either as a result of its dilapidated condition or the effects of the 'Beeching' cuts.

Shed-Codes

The Eastern Region was not issued with shed-codes at the outset of nationalisation in 1948 owing to BR's indecision over districts. In 1949 it was allocated ex-LMS type codes which followed on from the London Midland Region. Groups 30 to 33 represented the Stratford, Cambridge, Norwich and Plaistow areas respectively, whilst 40 to 46 considered for the remaining areas. (See list of shed-codes on page 104. These latter codes never materialised and the revised group 34 to 40 were decided upon later in the year.

Allocations

Where the depot's lifetime allows, three seperate allocations, of steam locomotives only, are listed from the years 1950, 1959 and 1965. There are a few exceptions to these years but they are confined to the minor sheds. The main lists are accurate to August 1950, April 1959 and May 1965.

Plans

All the plans have been based upon the Ordnance Survey County Series and National Grid maps from various years with the exception of the undermentioned. Reproduction is by permission of The Controller of Her Majesty's Stationery Office, Crown Copyright Reserved. 30C, 31A, 31B, 34A, 34D, 35A, 35B.

Photographs

All except 13 of the 117 illustrations have been restricted to the period 1948/66. The greater majority of the views are hitherto unpublished and represent many years of search.

30A STRATFORD

Pre-Grouping Origin: Great Eastern Railway
Gazetteer Ref: 40 B3
Closed: 1962
Shed-Code: 30A (1949 to 1962)
Allocations: 1950

Class B1 4-6-0
61000 *Springbok*
61001 *Eland*
61008 *Kudu*
61009 *Hartebeeste*

61089	61130	61192	61235	61360
61098	61144	61205	61236	61361
61104	61171	61227	61282	61362
61109	61175	61233	61335	61363
61119	61177	61234	61336	

Class B12 4-6-0

61514	61542	61567	61574	61580
61515	61546	61568	61575	
61516	61549	61571	61576	
61519	61550	61572	61578	
61525	61559	61573	61579	

Class B17 4-6-0
61602 *Walsingham*
61605 *Lincolnshire Regiment*
61606 *Audley End*
61608 *Gunton*
61610 *Honingham Hall*
61611 *Raynham Hall*
61612 *Houghton Hall*
61613 *Woodbastwick Hall*
61648 *Arsenal*
61654 *Sunderland*
61655 *Middlesbrough*
61658 *The Essex Regiment*

Class K2 2-6-0

61721	61745	61753	61761	61777
61734	61746	61754	61765	61778
61737	61752	61759	61767	61780

Class K3 2-6-0

61801	61815	61830	61835	61880
61805	61817	61831	61840	
61810	61820	61834	61849	

Class D16 4-4-0
62565

Class E4 2-4-0
62791

Class J19 0-6-0

64650	64652	64660	64663	64665
64651	64657	64662	64664	64670

Class J20 0-6-0

64675	64680	64685	64691
64676	64681	64686	64695
64677	64682	64690	64696

Class J39 0-6-0

64708	64767	64772	64776	64783
64764	64768	64773	64780	64874
64765	64769	64774	64781	64876
64766	64771	64775	64782	

Class J15 0-6-0

65361	65388	65450	65455	65466
65370	65440	65452	65463	65476
65384	65449	65453	65464	

Class J17 0-6-0

65500	65511	65528	65540	65543
65508	65523	65536	65541	

Class F5 2-4-2T

67192	67200	67206	67210	67214
67193	67202	67207	67211	
67197	67203	67208	67212	
67198	67205	67209	67213	

Class G5 0-4-4T

67269	67279	67322

Class L1 2-6-4T

67701	67723	67728	67733	67738
67712	67724	67729	67734	67739
67713	67725	67730	67735	
67721	67726	67731	67736	
67722	67727	67732	67737	

Class Y7 0-4-0T
68088S

Class Y4 0-4-0T

68125	68126	68127	68128	68129S

Class Y3 0-4-0T
68174

Class J66 0-6-0T

68370S	68380

Classes J67* and J69 0-6-0T

68491	68521*	68554	68589*	68613
68496*	68523*	68563	68590*	68617
68500	68526	68569	68591*	68619
68507	68527	68571	68592*	68621
68508	68532	68573	68594*	68626
68510*	68534	68574	68601	68631
68513*	68538	68575	68606*	68633
68517*	68546	68576	68607	68636
68519*	68548	68577	68608*	
68520*	68549	68588*	68612	

Class J68 0-6-0T

68638	68646	68650	68662
68639	68647	68652	68663
68642	68648	68660	68665
68644	68649	68661	68666

Class J92 0-6-0 Crane Tank

68667S	68668S	68669S

Class J50 0-6-0T

68950	68963	68965	68967	68977

Class N7 0-6-2T

69600	69627	69653	69674	69712
69601	69628	69654	69675	69713
69602	69629	69655	69676	69714
69603	69630	69656	69678	69715
69604	69631	69657	69680	69716
69605	69633	69658	69681	69717
69606	69634	69659	69682	69718
69607	69636	69660	69683	69719
69608	69637	69661	69684	69720
69609	69638	69662	69685	69721
69610	69641	69663	69686	69722
69611	69642	69664	69687	69723
69616	69643	69665	69688	69724
69617	69645	69666	69693	69725
69618	69646	69667	69697	69727
69619	69647	69668	69699	69728
69622	69648	69669	69700	69729
69623	69649	69670	69702	69730
69624	69650	69671	69704	69731
69625	69651	69672	69705	69732
69626	69652	69673	69710	69733

Total 383

@ 1950

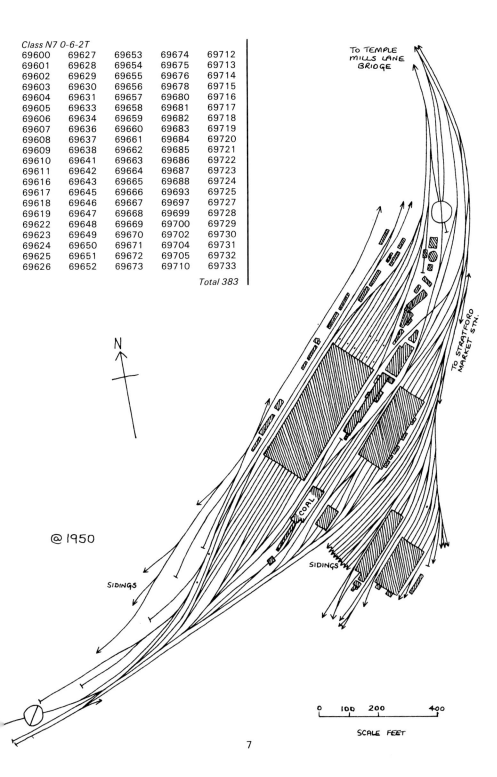

N

TO TEMPLE
MILLS LANE
BRIDGE

TO STRATFORD
MARKET STN.

COAL

SIDINGS

SIDINGS

0	100	200		400

SCALE FEET

7

Allocation: 1959

Class 4 2-6-0
43105	43148	43150
43144	43149	43151

Class 3F 0-6-0T
47282	47306	47311

Class B1 4-6-0
61089	61119	61233	61329	61367
61109	61164	61234	61335	61375

Class K5 2-6-0
61863

Class K1 2-6-0
62013	62015	62036
62014	62019	62053

Class J19 0-6-0
64653	64655	64656	64663	64670

Class J20 0-6-0
64675	64677	64681	64686	64693
64676	64680	64682	64689	64694

Class J39 0-6-0
64708	64767	64780	64787	64873
64750	64768	64781	64788	64973
64765	64773	64783	64799	
64766	64775	64784	64805	

Class J15 0-6-0
65361	65449	65455	65464
65440	65452	65463	65476

Class J17 0-6-0
65546	65548	65555	65563

Class L1 2-6-4T
67702	67709	67726	67731	67739
67703	67715	67727	67732	67752
67704	67716	67728	67735	67778
67706	67724	67729	67736	
67708	67725	67730	67737	

Class J69 0-6-0T
68500	68549	68577	68612
68513	68563	68578	68613
68526	68571	68596	68619
68538	68575	68600	68633

Class J68 0-6-0T
68644	68648	68652	68663
68646	68649	68655	68665
68647	68650	68660	

Class N7 0-6-2T
69602	69646	69665	69701	69721
69603	69647	69668	69702	69722
69604	69651	69670	69705	69723
69611	69653	69671	69708	69724
69614	69655	69674	69709	69725
69615	69656	69677	69710	69726
69620	69657	69679	69711	69728
69622	69658	69690	69712	69729
69626	69660	69691	69714	69730
69630	69661	69696	69715	
69636	69662	69697	69718	
69642	69663	69699	69719	
69645	69664	69700	69720	

Class 4 2-6-0
76030	76031	76032	76033	76034

Class WD 2-8-0
90028	90129	90298	90498	90551
90062	90156	90480	90508	90660

Total 197

A glance at the allocations will verify that this was the largest shed in the British Isles. In 1950 the shed could boast a total of 105 Class N7 locos from a possible 134.

At closure in September 1962 the remaining serviceable engines were transferred to 31B March.

Looking towards Stratford's coaling plant in June 1946 with 0-6-0T 'J67' No 8592 (later 68592) on the right. W. Potter

Class J66 0-6-0T No 68370S (Departmental No 32) outside the Service Shed at Stratford in 1953. These engines were responsible for the shunting movements in and about the nearby Stratford Works. B. Hilton

8

30B HERTFORD EAST

Pre-Grouping Origin: Great Eastern Railway
Gazetteer Ref: 11 F2
Closed: 1960
Shed-Code: 30B (1949 to 1960)
Allocations: 1952

Class J20 0-6-0
64699

Class N7 0-6-2T

69633	69681	69684	69687
69634	69682	69685	69688
69680	69683	69686	69693

Total 13

Allocations: 1959

Class N7 0-6-2T

69633	69681	69683	69685	69688
69680	69682	69684	69687	69693

Total 10

The shed was demolished in 1961.

As a result of the electrification scheme, Hertford East closed in November 1960 and had its allocation take over by Stratford 30A. Towards the end of its existence, the depot was regarded as being a sub-shed to Stratford.

Looking west into Hertford East shed in 1958 with 'N7' No 69702 (30A) just visible inside. K. Fairey

@ 1923

HERTFORD STN.
(G.E.R.)   GOODS   → WARE

N ↑

0   100   200   400
FEET

9

30C BISHOPS STORTFORD

Pre-Grouping Origin: Great Eastern Railway
Gazetteer Ref: 11 E3
Closed: 1960
Shed-Code: 30C (1949 to 1959)
Allocations: 1952 (30C)

Class J17 0-6-0
65528   65543

Class L1 2-6-4T
67713   67738

Class N7 0-6-2T
69713

Total 5

Looking north from the station footbridge in 1956 with a variety of tank classes in evidence at Bishops Stortford. Real Photos

Allocations: 1959 (31A sub)

Class J17 0-6-0
65528   65540   65556

Class L1 2-6-4T
67701   67718   67721   67733
67712   67720   67722   67734

Total 11

In 1959 the depot became a sub of 31A Cambridge. This open air depot lost its last duties in November 1960 to diesel traction. Locos were stored both sides of the main line because of the cramped space — the 'shed' was little more than a siding and a turntable! As such, many locos could be found on the approach roads to the goods shed.

Any record of a building ever having existed on this site has not been traced. A map of 1898 shows the layout as being almost identical to that of the one illustrated.

A 1958 view looking south from Bishop Stortford's station footbridge showing the forced accommodation of the sidings opposite to the 'shed'. The loco nearest the camera is Class J20 0-6-0 No 64683, a Cambridge engine.   K. Fairey

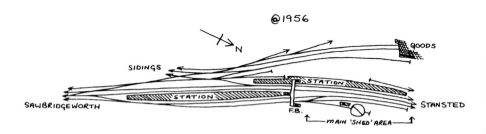

@ 1956

N

SIDINGS

GOODS

SAWBRIDGEWORTH

STATION

STATION

F.B.

STANSTED

MAIN 'SHED' AREA

FEET   0   100   200   400

30D SOUTHEND VICTORIA

Pre-Grouping Origin: Great Eastern Railway
Gazetteer Ref: 6 A4
Closed: 1957
Shed-Code: 30D (1949 to 1957)
Allocations: 1954

Class 3P 4-4-2T
41936* 41951* 41970* 41976*
41944* 49152* 41975*

Class B1 4-6-0
61329* 61336 61361 61363 61372*
61335 61360 61362 61370*

Class B12 4-6-0
61516* 61546* 61575* 61578*
61519* 61573* 61576*

Class J20 0-6-0
64675* 64676* 64677* 64680* 64681*

Class J69 0-6-0T
68534

Class N7 0-6-2T
69618 69645* 69712* 69725*

Total 33

Southend Victoria, although having a code of its own was regarded as a sub-depot to Stratford 30A. This is substantiated by the above group of engines, reported as being Southend's allocation in 1954. Those marked (*) were officially recognised as belonging to 30A yet a great number displayed 30D shed-code plates! (See photo.)

By 1956 the depot lost its allocation completely but continued with engines on loan until 1957 when electrification of the area put paid to steam's contribution.

For some years after closure the shed was used for loco storage.

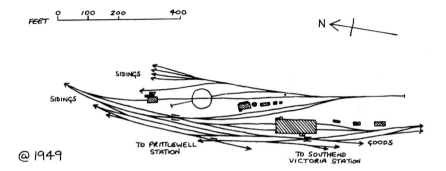

FEET 0 100 200 400

N

@ 1949

SIDINGS

SIDINGS

TO PRITTLEWELL STATION

TO SOUTHEND VICTORIA STATION

GOODS

A view of Class J20 No 64681 on shed at Southend Victoria in 1955. Whilst it can clearly be seen displaying a 30D shed-code plate, the locomotive was at this time on 30A Stratford's books. (See shed-notes). P. J. Kelley

An overall view of the Victoria site in the same year with Class N7 0-6-2T No 69725 alongside the coaler. H. C. Casserley

30E COLCHESTER

Pre-Grouping Origin: Great Eastern Railway
Gazetteer Ref: 12 E4
Closed: 1959
Shed-Code: 30E (1949 to 1959)
Allocations: 1950

Class B12 4-6-0
61512	61555	61557
61523	61556	61558

Class B2 and B17* 4-6-0
61603 *Framlingham*	61616 *Fallodon*
61607 *Blickling*	61632 *Belvoir Castle*
61614 *Castle Hedingham*	61639 *Norwich City*
61615 *Culford Hall*	61644* *Earlham Hall*

Class D16 4-4-0
62572	62598	62608

Class J15 0-6-0
65369	65431	65444	65454	65473
65402	65432	65445	65456	
65424	65441	65446	65465	
65427	65443	65448	65468	

Class J17 0-6-0
65522	65531	65539	65564

Class F5 2-4-2T
67188	67191	67196	67217
67189	67194	67204	67219
67190	67195	67215	

Class J70 0-6-0T
68226

Classes J67 and J69* 0-6-0T
68522	68578*	68616	68629*	68630*

Class N7 0-6-2T
69701	69726

Class WD 2-8-0
90029	90304	90443	90477	90522
90085	90431	90471	90508	90732

Total 67

Allocations: 1959

Class 4 2-6-0
43152	43153

Class 2 2-6-0
46468	46469

Class B1 4-6-0
61000 *Springbok*	61361
61300	61363
61311	61370
61336	61373

Class B17 4-6-0
61658 *The Essex Regiment*
61662 *Manchester United*
61663 *Everton*
61666 *Nottingham Forest*
61668 *Bradford City*

Class J19 0-6-0
64650	64660	64666
64657	64664	64667

Class J15 0-6-0
65424	65445	65448	65468	65472
65443	65446	65465	65470	65473

Class J17 0-6-0
65503	65506	65514	65539	65564
65505	65511	65531	65545	

Class J69 0-6-0T
68552	68573	68579

Class N7 0-6-2T
69612	69617	69673	69686	69732
69613	69652	69678	69727	69733

Total 55

At closure in December 1959 the displaced locos were moved to 30A Stratford. The shed buildings were demolished in 1961.

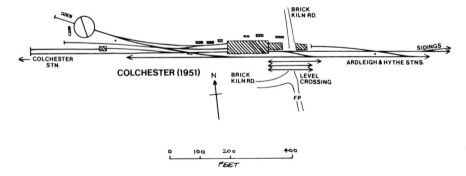

COLCHESTER (1951)

12

Colchester shed in 1951, looking east.   W. Potter

Colchester in 1959, a few months before closure.
The appearance of the electrification gantries in this
latter view suggests the main cause of closure was
modernisation.   K. Fairey

30F PARKESTON

Pre-Grouping Origin: Great Eastern Railway
Gazetteer Ref: 12 E3
Closed: 1961
Shed-Code: 30F (1949 to 1961)
Allocations: 1950

Class B1 4-6-0

61003 *Gazelle*	61006 *Blackbuck*	61226
61004 *Oryx*	61135	61232
61005 *Bongo*	61149	61264

Class J39 0-6-0

64770	64779	64788	64953
64777	64787	64873	

Class J15 0-6-0

65354	65434	65458

Class J69 0-6-0T

68556	68557	68561	68596

Class J68 0-6-0T

68643	68653

Class N7 0-6-2T

69612	69614	69621	69635	69677

Total 30

Parkeston shed in 1949 looking north to a group of locos sporting early BR livery. Real Photos

Allocations: 1959

Class B1 4-6-0

61003 *Gazelle*	61227
61004 *Oryx*	61232
61005 *Bongo*	61249 *FitzHerbert Wright*
61006 *Blackbuck*	61264
61111	61362
61135	61372
61149	61378
61226	61384

Class K3 2-6-0

61815	61862	61942	61963
61820	61921	61951	61977

Class J19 0-6-0
64652

Class J39 0-6-0

64776	64777

Class J15 0-6-0

65434	65453	65458

Class J68 0-6-0T
68643

Class N7 0-6-2T

69672	69675

Total 33

An important aspect of Parkeston's existence was the role it played servicing those locos which worked the Harwich boat trains. Its allocation of named Class B1s was therefore a mark of the depot's stature.

At closure in January 1961, the bulk of its locos went to 30A Stratford, but others went to 40E Colwick, 40A Lincoln and 41A Sheffield Darnall.

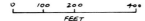

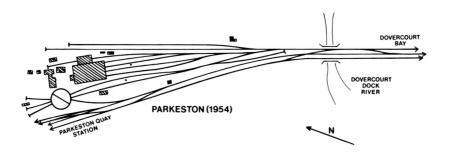

PARKESTON (1954)

DOVERCOURT BAY

DOVERCOURT DOCK RIVER

PARKESTON QUAY STATION

N

A prewar view of Parkeston depot in 1935. Photomatic

31A CAMBRIDGE

Pre-Grouping Origin: Great Eastern Railway
Gazetteer Ref: 11 C3
Closed: 1962
Shed-Code: 31A (1949 to 1962)
Allocations: 1950

Class B1 4-6-0

61121	61286	61300	61302	61334
61285	61287	61301	61333	

Classes B2* and B17 4-6-0

61617* *Ford Castle*
61619 *Welbeck Abbey*   61631 *Serlby Hall*
61620 *Clumber*   61636 *Harlaxton Manor*
61621 *Hatfield House*   61637 *Thorpe Hall*
61622 *Alnwick Castle*   61638 *Melton Hall*
61623 *Lambton Castle*   61640 *Somerleyton Hall*
61624 *Lumley Castle*   61642 *Kilverstone Hall*
61625 *Raby Castle*   61643 *Champion Lodge*
61627 *Aske Hall*   61663 *Everton*
61628 *Harewood House*   61671* *Royal Sovereign*

Class D16 4-4-0

62516	62530	62551	62571
62525	62531	62557	62574
62527	62549	62567	62618

Class E4 2-4-0

62781	62784	62788	62794
62783	62785	62790	

Class J20 0-6-0

64678	64679	64683	64684	64687

Class J15 0-6-0

65350	65405	65425	65457	65475
65356	65406	65438	65461	65477
65391	65413	65451	65474	

Class J17 0-6-0

65501	65520	65537	65563	65587
65502	65525	65538	65565	65589
65503	65529	65546	65573	
65506	65532	65547	65575	
65517	65535	65561	65585	

Class F6 2-4-2T
67222

Class C12 4-4-2T

67360	67367	67375	67385

Class J66 0-6-0T
68372   68383

Classes J67 and J69* 0-6-0T

68509	68516	68530*	68579*	68609

Class J68 0-6-0T
68645

Total 101

Allocations: 1959

Class 4 2-6-0
43087

Class 2 2-6-0
46465   46466   46467

Class B1 4-6-0

61066	61182	61280	61287	61360
61104	61203	61283	61301	61371
61171	61236	61286	61314	

Class B12 4-6-0
61577

Classes B2* and B17 4-6-0
61607 *Blickling*
61608 *Gunton*   61639* *Norwich City*
61613 *Woodbastwick Hall*   61644* *Earlham Hall*
61614* *Castle Hedingham*   61651 *Derby County*
61616* *Fallodon*   61652 *Darlington*
61623 *Lambton Castle*   61661 *Sheffield Wednesday*

Class K3 2-6-0

61817	61834	61849	61880

Class E4 2-4-0
62785

Class J19 0-6-0

64646	64654	64658	64661	64673

Class J20 0-6-0

64683	64695	64696

Class J39 0-6-0
64803   64985

Class J15 0-6-0

65450	65457	65475
65451	65461	65477

Class J17 0-6-0

65502	65528	65541	65580
65520	65532	65556	65589

Class L1 2-6-4T

67701	67713	67720	67722	67733
67712	67718	67721	67723	67734

Class J69 0-6-0T
68566   68609

Total 71

Closure in June 1962 resulted in the remaining locos being moved to 31B March and 30A Stratford.

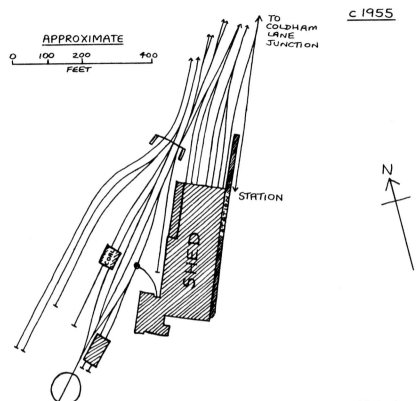

c 1955

APPROXIMATE

0   100   200   400
└────────────────────┘
        FEET

TO
COLDHAM
LANE
JUNCTION

STATION

SHED

COAL

N ↗

Note: Extensive search has failed to locate a plan of the remodelled 31A (rebuilt by the LNER in 1932). The layout illustrated has been formulated from photos, sketches and the recollections of Shed-staff from the 1950's period. It must therefore be pointed out that this plan is *not to scale* and that the track geometry may not be wholly correct.

An overall view of Cambridge shed in 1960. The station can be seen on the extreme left.   W. Potter

17

31B March

Pre-Grouping Origin: Great Eastern Railway
Gazetteer Ref: 17 F3
Closed: 1963
Shed-Code: 31B (1949 to 1963)
Allocations: 1950

Class B17 4-6-0
61626 *Brancepeth Castle*
61630 *Tottenham Hotspur*
61633 *Kimbolton Castle*
61635 *Milton*
61641 *Gayton Hall*
61646 *Gilwell Park*
61656 *Leeds United*
61660 *Hull City*
61666 *Nottingham Forest*
61672 *West Ham United*

Class K3 2-6-0

61844	61864	61886	61893	61946
61846	61866	61887	61895	61948
61847	61869	61888	61938	61961
61860	61873	61889	61940	

Class K1 2-6-0

62011	62017	62033	62039	62055
62012	62018	62034	62040	62066
62013	62019	62035	62051	62067
62014	62020	62036	62052	62068
62015	62031	62037	62053	62069
62016	62032	62038	62054	62070

Class D16 4-4-0

62529	62542	62548	62589	62605
62539	62547	62579	62603	

Class O4 2-8-0

63701	63704	63730	63897

Class J19 0-6-0

64641	64648	64659	64667
64643	64655	64661	64669
64647	64656	64666	64671

Class J20 0-6-0

64688	64692	64694	64698
64689	64693	64697	64699

Class J15 0-6-0

65366	65439

Class J17 0-6-0

65505	65521	65556	65577
65515	65554	65571	65583
65518	65555	65576	65584

Class F4 2-4-2T

67153	67187

Class J68 0-6-0T

68654	68664

Class Q1 0-8-0T

69926

Class WD 2-8-0

90003	90053	90175	90425	90510
90005	90055	90221	90433	90519
90013	90060	90224	90442	90540
90015	90064	90275	90453	90580
90018	90066	90294	90473	90582
90023	90083	90302	90474	90601
90024	90087	90384	90476	90602
90035	90118	90392	90480	90608
90037	90119	90393	90502	90660
90042	90131	90422	90506	90668

Total 161

Allocations: 1959

Class V2 2-6-2

60803	60830	60858	60938	60948

Class B17 4-6-0
61610 *Honingham Hall*
61626 *Brancepeth Castle*
61627 *Aske Hall*
61633 *Kimbolton Castle*
61641 *Gayton Hall*
61653 *Huddersfield Town*
61657 *Doncaster Rovers*

Class K3 2-6-0

61801	61827	61845	61890	61948
61810	61831	61860	61915	61954
61811	61835	61861	61929	61972
61822	61840	61886	61946	61976

Class K1 2-6-0

62016	62032	62038	62054	62068
62017	62033	62039	62055	62069
62018	62035	62040	62066	62070
62020	62037	62051	62067	

Class D16 4-4-0

62529	62589	62618

Class O1 2-8-0

63571	63646	63678	63780	63868
63590	63650	63687	63784	63872
63596	63652	63725	63786	63879
63619	63663	63746	63795	63887
63630	63670	63773	63803	63890

Class J19 0-6-0

64642	64648	64665	64669
64647	64659	64668	64671

Class J20 0-6-0

64678	64684	64690	64692	64698
64679	64687	64691	64697	64699

Class J39 0-6-0

64764	64770	64772	64779
64769	64771	64774	64782

Class J15 0-6-0

65420	65474

Class J17 0-6-0

65554	65576	65577	65583	65584

'Britannia' 4-6-2
70035 *Rudyard Kipling*

Class WD 2-8-0

90001	90079	90208	90340	90683
90018	90083	90279	90477	90709
90023	90150	90293	90484	
90042	90191	90305	90522	

Total 131

By closure in November 1963, March had acquired a number of 'Britannia' Pacifics which were then transferred to the London Midland Region. The remainder of the depot's serviceable locos went to 41H Staveley Central.

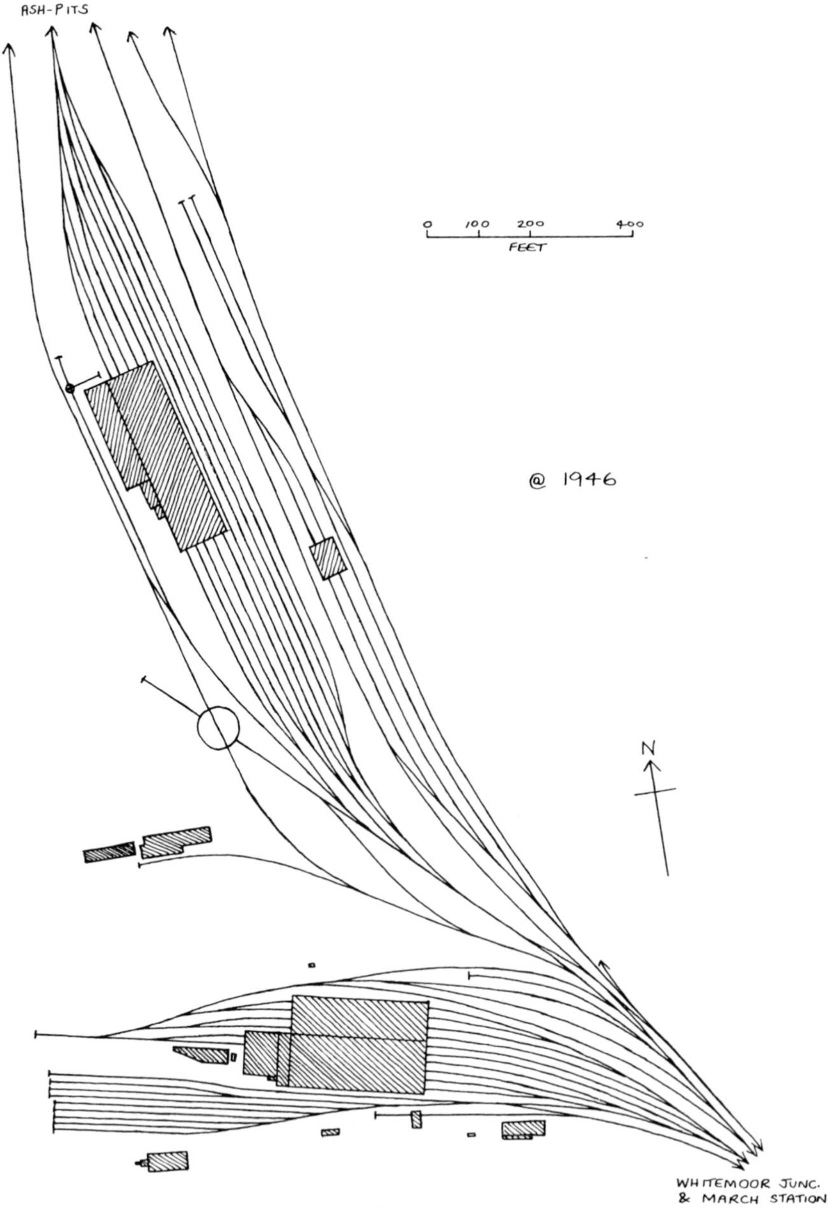

ASH-PITS

@ 1946

N

WHITEMOOR JUNC.
& MARCH STATION

Class D16 4-4-0 No 62618 (31A) simmers outside
its home depot in May 1957.   K. Fairey

Looking south to the through-road building (wash
out shed) at March in 1960. The number of locos in
steam indicates the strategical importance of the
depot.   K. Fairey

This view of March from Whitemoor Junction shows
the engine shed approaches on the left with the
wash out shed and coaling tower in the distance on
the right hand side. (Also taken in 1960).   W. Potter

31C KINGS LYNN

Pre-Grouping Origin: Great Eastern Railway
Gazetteer Ref: 17 E4
Closed: 1959
Shed-Code: 31C (1949 to 1959)
Allocations: 1950

Classes D15* and D16 4-4-0

62501*	62506*	62514	62569	62601
62502*	62507*	62518	62575	62614
62505*	62513	62559	62582	

Class J19 0-6-0

64640	64642	64654	64668	64672

Class J15 0-6-0

65359	65378	65437

Class J17 0-6-0

65519	65530	65544	65549
65527	65542	65548	65572

Class F6 2-4-2T

67221	67227

Class Y6 0-4-0T

68082	68083

Class J70 0-6-0T

68217	68220	68222	68223	68225

Classes J67* and J69 0-6-0T

68490*	68494	68514*	68545
68493*	68502	68515*	

Class J68 0-6-0T

68656

Total 47

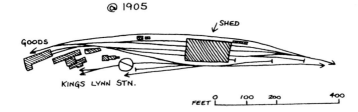

@ 1905

SHED

GOODS

KINGS LYNN STN.

N

FEET 0 100 200 400

*Looking east to Kings Lynn depot in August 1959.
The presence of 0-6-0 No 44522 (31F) in steam four
months after dieselisation proves that this and many
other 'closed to steam' depots serviced and turned
the odd visitor from steam sheds.   L. Hanson*

Allocations: 1959

Class 4 2-6-0
43089   43090   43094

Class B17 4-6-0
61620 *Clumber*

Class D16 4-4-0
62606

Class J19 0-6-0
64640

The other end of Kings Lynn shed in 1953 with Class D16 4-4-0 No 62579 (31C) outside. B. K. B. Green

Class J17 0-6-0

65521	65530	65544	65565
65526	65533	65549	65582

Class J69 0-6-0T
68499   68542

Class N7 0-6-2T
69694

Total 17

At steam closure in April 1959 the displaced engines were transferred to South Lynn 31D to supplement that depot's two Ivatt Moguls. (See 31D.)

The shed was demolished in the year of complete closure, 1961.

31D SOUTH LYNN

Pre-Grouping Origin: Midland & Great Northern Railway
Gazetteer Ref: 17 E4
Closed: 1959
Shed-Code: 31D (1949 to 1959)
Allocations: 1950

Class B12 4-6-0
61533   61537   61540   61547

Class K2 2-6-0
61738   61743   61757
61742   61748   61766

Class D16 4-4-0
62534   62543   62558   62573

Class J19 0-6-0
64645   64649   64658
64646   64653   64673

Class J17 0-6-0
65504   65533   65562   65580   65588
65526   65545   65579   65582

Class J66 0-6-0T
68378

Classes J67* and J69 0-6-0T
68542   68566   68597*   68600

Total 34

Although closing in February 1959, it was reported that two Ivatt Moguls (43xxx) were kept at the depot for some time after and that these were added to in April of the same year by the influx of displaced locos from the ex-GER depot at Kings Lynn (31C) which closed to steam in that month.

The previously mentioned 43xxx class formed the mainstay of South Lynn's allocation towards the end with 17 locos being stationed there in 1958. (Nos 43068/90-95/104/5/7-11/42-44.)

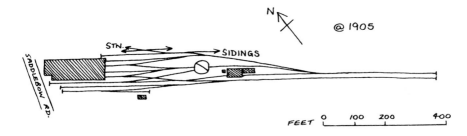

A north-westerly view of South Lynn depot in the mid-1950s. The two engines astride the water-columns are: (left to right) Class J17 0-6-0 No 65514 and Class 4MT 2-6-0 No 43142. B. Yale

The rebuilt South Lynn shed in February 1959, the month of closure, with Class 4MT 2-6-0s (left to right) 43157, 43111 and 43093. T. Wright

31E BURY ST EDMUNDS

Pre-Grouping Origin: Great Eastern Railway
Gazetteer Ref: 12 C5
Closed: 1959
Shed-Code: 31E (1949 to 1959)
Allocations: 1950

Classes D15* and D16 4-4-0
62503*   62508*   62566   62607   62615

Class E4 2-4-0
62786   62795

Class J15 0-6-0
65362   65420   65442

Class F6 2-4-2T
67236   67237   67238

Class J69 0-6-0T
68497

Total 14

In 1959 it was reported that this depot had long been regarded as a sub of 31A Cambridge with unofficial transfers between the two having taken place. The shed closed in January 1959 and the locos, not surprisingly, found themselves moved to Cambridge.

@ 1926

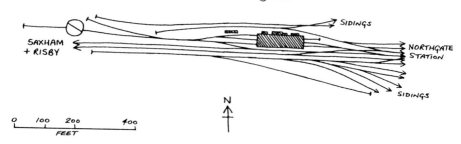

A view of the east end of Bury St Edmund's shed in 1957, with 'B12' No 61555 (31A).   K. Fairey

32A NORWICH

Pre-Grouping Origin: Great Eastern Railway
Gazetteer Ref: 18 F3
Closed: 1962
Shed-Code: 32A (1949 to 1962)
Allocations: 1950

Class B1 4-6-0
61040 Roedeer

61041	61045	61049	61270
61042	61046	61050	61271
61043	61047	61051	61272
61044	61048	61052	61332

Class B17 4-6-0
61609 *Quidenham*
61629 *Naworth Castle*
61659 *East Anglian*
61670 *City of London*

Class K3 2-6-0

61921	61942	61953	61970	61981
61939	61947	61957	61971	61989

Class D16 4-4-0

62510	62552	62570	62593	62617
62522	62553	62577	62606	62619
62540	62554	62581	62610	
62541	62555	62584	62612	
62545	62556	62585	62616	

Class E4 2-4-0

62780	62787	62792	62796
62782	62789	62793	62797

Class J19 0-6-0
64644   64674

Class J39 0-6-0

64724	64761	64802	64889	64968
64726	64784	64833	64913	
64731	64797	64882	64959	

Class J15 0-6-0

65373	65404	65426	65471
65390	65417	65460	65472
65398	65422	65469	65479

Class J17 0-6-0

65507	65514	65553	65570
65512	65524	65568	65574
65513	65534	65569	65578

Class F3 2-4-2T
67139

Class F4 2-4-2T
67176   67178

Class F6 2-4-2T
67229   67232

Class V1 2-6-2T

67663	67664	67677	67679

Class L1 2-6-4T

67788	67789	67794	67795	67798

Class J66 0-6-0T
68381   68388

Classes J67* and J69 0-6-0T

68495	68570	68602
68501	68586*	68603

Class J68 0-6-0T
68641

Class J50 0-6-0T
68899   68905   68924

Class N7 0-6-2T

69706	69707	69708	69709

Total 130

Allocations: 1959

Class 4 2-6-0

43145	43146	43156	43160	43161

Class B1 4-6-0

61042	61046	61235	61312
61043	61048	61270	61317
61045	61223	61279	61399

Class B12 4-6-0

61514	61530	61533	61568	61571

Class B17 4-6-0
61636 *Harlaxton Manor*
61654 *Sunderland*

Class K3 2-6-0

61826	61918	61953	61971	61989
61877	61939	61957	61973	
61908	61949	61970	61981	

Class D16 4-4-0

62511	62517	62524	62540	62544

Class J19 0-6-0

64641	64643	64644	64674

Class J39 0-6-0

64731	64761	64900	64913

Class J15 0-6-0
65469   65471

Class J17 0-6-0

65519	65551	65557	65570	65586
65542	65553	65566	65581	

Class L1 2-6-4T
67714   67717   67786

Class J68 0-6-0T
68640   68641   68645

Class J50 0-6-0T
68899   68905   68924

25

Class N7 0-6-2T
69107

'Britannia' 4-6-2
70000 *Britannia*
70001 *Lord Hurcomb*
70002 *Geoffrey Chaucer*
70003 *John Bunyan*
70005 *John Milton*
70006 *Robert Burns*
70007 *Couer-de-Lion*
70008 *Black Prince*
70009 *Alfred the Great*
70010 *Owen Glendower*
70011 *Hotspur*

70012 *John of Gaunt*
70013 *Oliver Cromwell*
70030 *William Wordsworth*
70034 *Thomas Hardy*
70036 *Boadicea*
70037 *Hereward the Wake*
70038 *Robin Hood*
70039 *Sir Christopher Wren*
70040 *Clive of India*
70041 *Sir John Moore*

Class WD 2-8-0
90559   *Total 93*

At closure in March 1962 the bulk of remaining
engines re-allocated to 31B March.

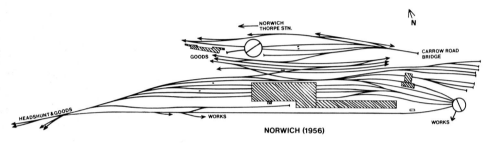

NORWICH (1956)

FEET

*Looking west to Norwich shed in the mid-1950s.
'Britannia' class 4-6-2 No 70008 Black Prince (32A)
can be seen in the centre, whilst to the left 'B12'
No 61568 (also 32A) offers a visual contrast in
express pasenger design spanning 40 years. B. Yale*

26

A more distant view of Norwich in 1956 with freight Classes J17 and J39 (Nos 65573 and 64761) nearest the camera.   W. Potter

32B IPSWICH

Pre-Grouping Origin: Great Eastern Railway
Gazetteer Ref: 12 D3
Closed: 1959
Shed-Code: 32B (1949 to 1959)
Allocations: 1950

Class 2MT 2-6-2T
41200

Class B1 4-6-0
61053	61055	61058	61201	61253
61054	61056	61059	61252	61254

Class B12 4-6-0
61535	61562	61566	61570
61561	61564	61569	61577

Class B17 4-6-0
61600 *Sandringham*	61645 *The Suffolk Regiment*
61601 *Holkham*	61647 *Helmingham Hall*
61604 *Elveden*	61649 *Sheffield United*
61618 *Wynyard Park*	61668 *Bradford City*
61634 *Hinchingbrooke*	61669 *Barnsley*

Class D16 4-4 0
62526   62590

Class J39 0-6-0
64752	64800	64826	64841	64905
64785	64803	64829	64894	64957
64793	64820	64834	64900	64958

Class J15 0-6-0
65377	65407	65429	65459
65382	65408	65430	65467
65396	65423	65447	65470

Class J17 0-6-0
65510   65560

Class F3 2-4-2T
67128

Class F6 2-4-2T
67220   67230   67239

Class L1 2-6-4T
67702	67705	67709	67716
67703	67706	67710	67719
67704	67708	67711	67787

Class J65 0-6-0T
68211

Class J70 0-6-0T
68216   68221   68224

Class J66 0-6-0T
68373   68374   68375

Class J67 0-6-0T
68498   68518   68593

Class J72 0-6-0T
69012   69013

Class N7 0-6-2T
69703   69711

Total 90

Allocations: 1959

Class B1 4-6-0
61001 *Eland*
61052	61056	61160	61253
61054	61058	61228	61254
61055	61059	61252	

Class B12 4-6-0
61535   61564   61572

Class B17 4-6-0
61611 *Raynham Hall*	61629 *Naworth Castle*
61612 *Houghton Hall*	61637 *Thorpe Hall*
61618 *Wynyard Park*	61647 *Helmingham Hall*
61625 *Raby Castle*	61672 *West Ham United*

Class J39 0-6-0
64724	64793	64829	64891
64752	64800	64834	64894
64785	64826	64841	64905

Class J15 0-6-0
65388	65389	65454	65459	65478

Class J17 0-6-0
65512	65513	65560	65561	65578

Class L1 2-6-4T
67705	67710	67711	67719	67775

Total 50

The shed was rebuilt in 1954 with a view towards future accommodation of diesels.

Although officially closing in November 1959, the last of its steam locos were not transferred away until April 1960. The other ex-GER shed at March took most of the redundant stock in 1959.

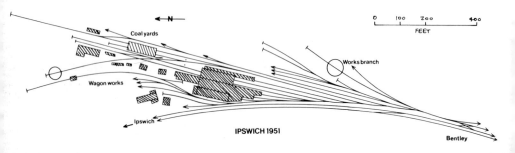

IPSWICH 1951

Ipswich in 1956 depicting the modern four road steam accommodation alongside the two road diesel structure. Locos Nos 65404 (32A) and 61629 Naworth Castle (32B) stand outside.   BR

A ground level view of Ipswich in the same year looking south.   N. E. Preedy

32C LOWESTOFT

Pre-Grouping Origin: Great Eastern Railway
Gazetteer Ref: 18 G1
Closed: 1960
Shed-Code: 32C (1949 to 1960)
Allocations: 1950

Class K3 2-6-0
61926   61949   61958   61959   61973

Class J15 0-6-0
65355   65389   65433   65462
65374   65401   65435   65478

Class J17 0-6-0
65566

Class F3 2-4-2T
67127

Class F4 2-4-2T
67156   67167   67186
67158   67174
67163   67177
67165   67182
67166   67184

Class F5 2-4-2T
67201   67216

Class F6 2-4-2T
67231

Class Y1 0-4-0T
68130S   68131S

Class Y3 0-4-0T
68168S   68173S   68177S   68178S

Class J67 0-6-0T
68611

Class J68 0-6-0T
68640

Total 37

Allocations: 1959

Class B17 4-6-0
61659 *East Anglian*
61660 *Hull City*

Class K3 2-6-0
61926   61958   61959

Class J39 0-6-0
64797

Class J15 0-6-0
65460   65462

Class J17 0-6-0
65558   65559   65567   65588

Class L1 2-6-4T
67707   67738

Class J69 0-6-0T
68565

Class J68 0-6-0T
68642

Class N7 0-6-2T
69621   69706

Total 18

At closure in September 1960, the Lowestoft engines were re-allocated to 32A Norwich.

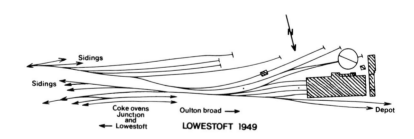

LOWESTOFT 1949

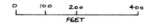

FEET

30

Lowestoft depot in 1956 with tank classes (left to right) 'J68' No 68664 and 'F6' No 67229 (both 32C) nearest the camera. N. E. Preedy

Looking west in 1951 prior to the rebuilding of the roof, the result of which is shown in the other view. The locos facing (Nos 67127 and 67184) are both of Lowestoft depot and of 'F4' 2-4-2T classification. N. E. Preedy

32D YARMOUTH SOUTH TOWN

Pre-Grouping Origin: Great Eastern Railway
Gazetteer Ref: 18 F1
Closed: 1959
Shed-Code: 32D (1949 to 1959)
Allocations: 1950

Class B17 4-6-0
61661 *Sheffield Wednesday*
61665 *Leicester City*

Class D16 4-4-0
62511	62580
62517	62586
62521	62597
62524	62604
62544	62611
62546 *Claud Hamilton*	62613
62576	

Class F4 2-4-2T
67154

Class F5 2-4-2T
67199

Class F6 2-4-2T
67218

Class Y10 0-4-0T
68186

Class J70 0-6-0T
68219

Classes J67* and J69 0-6-0T
68625   68628*

Total 22

Allocations: 1959

Class B17 4-6-0
61656 *Leeds United*
61664 *Liverpool*
61670 *City of London*

Class D16 4-4-0
62570   62604

Class J68 0-6-0T
68656

Total 6

At closure in November 1959, the remaining locos were moved to 32C Lowestoft.

South Town in February 1959 after rebuilding with two of its Class B17 allocation, Nos 61665 Leicester City *and 61670* City of London. *The former engine (inside the shed) was withdrawn soon after and is thus not included in the accompanying 1959 (April) listing.* T. Wright

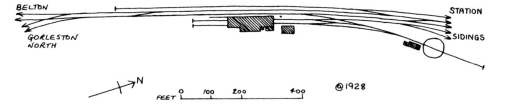

BELTON

STATION

GORLESTON
NORTH

SIDINGS

N

FEET   0   100   200   400   © 1928

Looking north to the dilapidated South Town shed in
1956. On view are (left to right) Classes C12 4-4-2T
No 67366 and B17 4-6-0 No 61622 Alnwick Castle
(both 32D).   W. Potter

32E YARMOUTH VAUXHALL

Class D16 62586 (32E) peers outside Vauxhall shed in 1953 looking north-east. Real Photos

Pre-Grouping Origin: Great Eastern Railway
Gazetteer Ref: 18 F1
Closed: 1959
Shed-Code: 32E (1949 to 1959)
Allocations: 1955

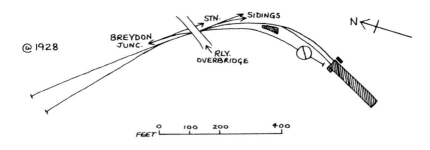

@ 1928

```
Class D16 4-4-0
62511    62524    62586    62613
62517    62580    62611

Class F4 2-4-2T
67162

Class J67 0-6-0T
68628
```
Total 9

In 1957 it was reported that this shed had begun being worked as a sub of 32D Yarmouth South Town although retaining its own code until closure in January 1959.

Two of Vauxhall shed's 'D16s' outside the building in 1956, (left to right) Nos 62613 and 62517.
N. E. Preedy

34

32F YARMOUTH BEACH

Pre-Grouping Origin: Midland & Great Northern
Railway
Gazetteer Ref: 18 F1
Closed: 1959
Shed-Code: 32F (1949 to 1959)
Allocations: 1950

Class B12 4-6-0
61520   61530   61545

Class D16 4-4-0
62561   62564   62592   62596

Class J17 0-6-0
65558   65559   65581

Class F6 2-4-2T
67223   67226   67233   67234   67235

Class J65 0-6-0T
68214

Class J68 0-6-0T
68651

Total 17

At closure in February 1959, one engine went to 40E
Colwick but the remainder were taken by 32A
Norwich.

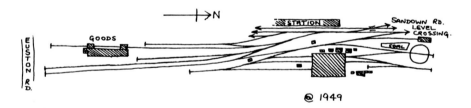

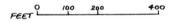

FEET

Class 4MT 2-6-0 No 43160 receiving attention outside Yarmouth Beach depot in the mid-1950s.
B. Yale

Looking north to Yarmouth Beach depot on 28 February 1959, the last day of steam operation, with No 43107 simmering outside. T. Wright

32G MELTON CONSTABLE

Pre-Grouping Origin: Midland & Great Northern Railway
Gazetteer Ref: 18 D4
Closed: 1959
Shed-Code: 32G (1949 to 1959)
Allocations: 1950

Classes D15* and D16 4-4-0

62509*	62520*	62533	62578
62515	62523	62538*	62620
62519	62528*	62562	

Class J17 0-6-0

65509	65551	65557	65586
65516	65552	65567	

Class F4 2-4-2T

67152	67162

Class F6 2-4-2T

67224	67225	67228

Class J66 0-6-0T
68377

Class J67 0-6-0T
68536

Class N7 0-6-2T
69679

Total 26

In 1951 the shed was reconstructed in brick after the collapse of the old wooden building in the same year. Upon closure in February 1959, the bulk of the locos went to 32A Norwich and 30A Stratford but others went to 30E Colchester, 40E Colwick and 40F Boston.

This 1958 view looking south-east shows Melton Constable station on the left and Class 4 locos Nos 43154 and 43147 (both 32G) alongside the shed building on the right.   A. G. Ellis

Melton Constable in the month of closure, February 1959, with Class 4 2-6-0s Nos 43152 and 43157 on view.   T. Wright

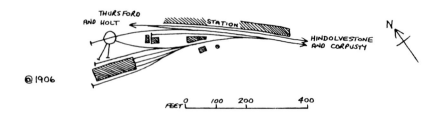

38

39

33A PLAISTOW

Pre-Grouping Origin: London, Tilbury & Southend Railway
Gazetteer Ref: 40 C2
Closed: 1962 (see below)
Shed-Codes: 13A (1948 to 1949)
33A (1949 to 1959)
Allocations: 1950

Class 2P 4-4-2T
41915

Class 3P 4-4-2T

41928	41937	41945	41965	41975
41929	41939	41948	41967	41976
41930	41941	41950	41968	41977
41931	41942	41951	41969	41978
41936	41944	41956	41970	

Class 3F 0-6-2T

41981	41984	41987	41990
41982	41985	41988	41993
41983	41986	41989	

Class 4MT 2-6-4T

42225	42249	42255	42531	42678
42226	42250	42256	52532	42679
42227	42251	42257	42533	42681
42231	42252	42328	42534	42684
42232	42253	42374	42535	42687
42248	42254	42530	42536	

Class 4F 0-6-0
44228   44530

Class 3F 0-6-0T

47300	47328	47458	47512
47311	47351	47484	

Class 1P 0-4-4T

58038	58043	58062	58065	58089

Class 2F 0-6-0

58184	58191	58259	58289

Total 83

Allocations: 1959

Class 3F 0-6-2T
41981

Class 4 2-6-4T

42226	42227	42254	42255	42257

Class 3F 0-6-0T

47262	47328	47484	47555
47312	47351	47512	

Class J39 0-6-0

64951	64953	64956	64958	64965
64952	64954	64957	64962	64968

Class 4 2-6-4T

80096	80100	80104	80133
80097	80101	80105	80134
80098	80102	80131	80135
80099	80103	80132	80136

Class WD 2-8-0
90196   90256   90653

Total 42

The depot became a sub-shed of 33B Tilbury in 1959 and although 'officially' closing in 1960 remained in use in this role until 1962.

At final closure in June 1962, the men were transferred to the Electric Depot at East Ham and the building was then used for the storage of condemned locos.

Originally the shed was London Midland Region property but it came under the Eastern Region's control in 1949 and took up the code 33A.

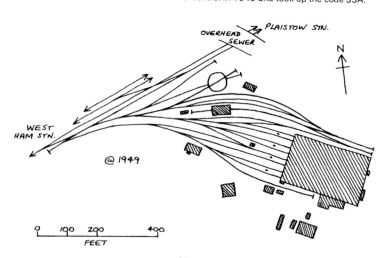

OVERHEAD SEWER

PLAISTOW STN.

N

WEST HAM STN.

@ 1949

0   100   200   400
FEET

40

Looking east to Plaistow shed in 1952 with an even blend of ex-LNER and ex-LMS locos.   W. Potter

This view of Plaistow in 1954 shows 'WD' class 2-8-0 No 90196 (36B), '35F' 0-6-0T No 47262 (33A), an unidentified '4MT' 2-6-4T and brand-new BR Class 4MT 2-6-4T No 80135 (33A).   C. I. K. Field

33B TILBURY

Pre-Grouping Origin: London, Tilbury & Southend Railway
Gazetteer Ref: 5 B5
Closed: 1962
Shed-Codes: 13C (1948 to 1949)
33B (1949 to 1962)
Allocations: 1950

Class 3P 4-4-2T
41932   41935   41952   41955
41933   41946   41953   41957
41934   41949   41954   41959

Class 3F 0-6-2T
41980

Class 4MT 2-6-4T
42218   42220   42222   42224
42219   42221   42223

Class 2F 0-6-0
58129

Total 21

Allocations: 1959

Class 4 2-6-4T
80069   80072   80075   80078
80070   80073   80076   80079
80071   80074   80077   80080

Class WD 2-8-0
90034   90106   90442   90514
90093   90244   90494

Total 19

In 1949 Tilbury transferred to the Eastern Region's control from the London Midland Region.

In June 1962 the depot lost its allocation and became regarded as a sub shed to 30A Stratford. The engines transferred to the Western Region and Stratford.

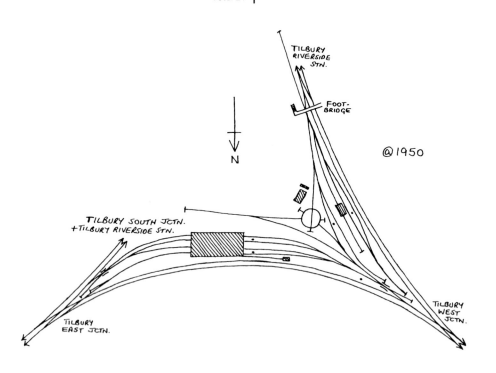

42

Tilbury in 1961 with Class WD No 90522 and Class 4 No 80105 (both 33B) outside the depot. As will be seen from the allocations these two types dominated the scene at Tilbury during its last years. K. Fairey

An earlier view of Tilbury with Class 4 2-6-4T No 80071 at the head of a line of locos inside the depot. Real Photos

33C SHOEBURYNESS

Pre-Grouping Origin: London, Tilbury & Southend Railway
Gazetteer Ref: 6 A4
Closed: 1962
Shed-Codes: 13D (1948 to 1949)
33C (1949 to 1962)
Allocations: 1950

Class 3P 4-4-2T

41960	41963	41964	41966

Class 3F 0-6-2T

41991	41992

Class 4MT 2-6-4T

42500	42506	42512	42518	42524
42501	42507	42513	42519	42525
42502	42508	42514	42520	42526
42503	42509	42515	42521	42527
42504	42510	42516	42522	42528
42505	42511	42517	42523	42529

Total 36

Allocations: 1959

Class 4 2-6-4T

42218	42504	42514	42524	42534
42219	42505	42515	42525	42535
42220	42506	42516	42526	42536
42221	42507	42517	42527	42678
42223	42508	42518	42528	42679
42224	42509	42519	42529	42681
42500	42510	42520	42530	42684
42501	42511	42521	42531	42687
42502	42512	42522	42532	
42503	42513	42523	42533	

Total 48

It will be seen that the entire class of Stanier 3-cylinder Class 4 2-6-4Ts introduced in 1934 for the LTSR line were shedded at Shoeburyness in 1959. (Nos 42500-36 inclusive.)

The shed transferred to the Eastern Region in 1949 and became 33C.

At closure in June 1962 most of the engines were withdrawn but a few did transfer to the London Midland Region.

Looking east to Shoeburyness shed from the station in 1954. On view are Class 4 42509 (33C) and BR standard Class 4 80076 (33A). Photomatic

Class 4 2-6-4Ts Nos 42505 and 42678 in steam at Shoeburyness in 1961 (both 33C). K. Fairey

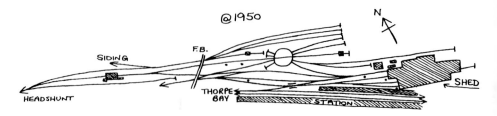

44

34A KINGS CROSS

Pre-Grouping Origin: Great Northern Railway
Gazetteer Ref: 40 B5
Closed: 1963
Shed-Code: 34A (1949 to 1963)
Allocations: 1950

Class A4 4-6-2
60003 *Andrew K. McCosh*
60006 *Sir Ralph Wedgwood*
60007 *Sir Nigel Gresley*
60008 *Dwight D. Eisenhower*
60010 *Dominion of Canada*
60013 *Dominion of New Zealand*
60014 *Silver Link*
60017 *Silver Fox*
60021 *Wild Swan*
60022 *Mallard*
60025 *Falcon*
60028 *Walter K. Whigham*
60029 *Woodcock*
60030 *Golden Fleece*
60032 *Gannet*
60033 *Seagull*
60034 *Lord Faringdon*

Class A3 4-6-2
60039 *Sandwich*	60089 *Felstead*
60059 *Tracery*	60105 *Victor Wild*
60063 *Isinglass*	60108 *Gay Crusader*
60065 *Knight of Thistle*	60109 *Hermit*
60067 *Ladas*	60110 *Robert the Devil*

Class A1 4-6-2
60122 *Curlew*	60144 *King's Courier*
60128 *Bongrace*	60148 *Aboyeur*
60130 *Kestrel*	60149 *Amadis*
60131 *Osprey*	60156 *Great Central*
60136 *Alcazar*	60157 *Great Eastern*
60139 *Sea Eagle*	60158 *Aberdonian*

Class W1 4-6-4
60700

Class V2 2-6-2
60800 *Green Arrow*	60900
60813	60903
60814	60909
60821	60914
60823	60915
60862	60922
60873 *Coldstreamer*	60983
60892	

Class B1 4-6-0
61113	61139
61129	61200
61136	61203
61137	61251 *Oliver Bury*
61138	61266

Class F2 2-4-2T
67111

Class C12 4-4-2T
67356	67374

Class L1 2-6-4T
67792	67793	67796	67797

Class J52 0-6-0ST
68764	68799	68822	68854	68874
68770	68802	68828	68855	68878
68771	68803	68830	68861	68881
68772	68805	68831	68862	68884
68780	68809	68832	68864	68888
68797	68818	68838	68873	68889

Class N2 0-6-2T
69490	69519	69536	69561	69579
69491	69520	69538	69568	69581
69492	69521	69539	69569	69583
69495	69523	69540	69570	69584
69496	69524	69541	69571	69585
69497	69525	69542	69572	69589
69498	69526	69543	69573	69590
69499	69527	69544	69574	69591
69502	69528	69545	69575	69592
69506	69529	69546	69576	69593
69512	69532	69548	69577	
69517	69535	69549	69578	

Total 160

Allocations: 1959

Class A4 4-6-2
60003 *Andrew K. McCosh*
60006 *Sir Ralph Wedgwood*
60007 *Sir Nigel Gresley*
60008 *Dwight D. Eisenhower*
60010 *Dominion of Canada*
60013 *Dominion of New Zealand*
60014 *Silver Link*
60015 *Quicksilver*
60017 *Silver Fox*
60021 *Wild Swan*
60022 *Mallard*
60025 *Falcon*
60026 *Miles Beevor*
60028 *Walter K. Whigham*
60029 *Woodcock*
60030 *Golden Fleece*
60032 *Gannet*
60033 *Seagull*
60034 *Lord Faringdon*

Class A3 4-6-2
60039 *Sandwich*	60062 *Minoru*
60044 *Melton*	60066 *Merry Hampton*
60055 *Woolwinder*	60103 *Flying Scotsman*
60059 *Tracery*	60109 *Hermit*
60061 *Pretty Polly*	60110 *Robert the Devil*

Class V2 2-6-2
60800 *Green Arrow*
60814	60854	60871	60903	60950
60820	60862	60902	60914	60983

46

Class B1 4-6-0
61075	61179	61272	61364	61394
61174	61200	61331	61393	

Class L1 2-6-4T
67757	67772	67779	67787	67800
67767	67773	67780	67792	
67768	67774	67783	67793	
67770	67776	67784	67797	

Class J52 0-6-0ST
68846

Class J50 0-6-0T
68946

Class N2 0-6-2T
69490	69520	69535	69568	69581
69492	69521	69538	69570	69583
69498	69523	69539	69574	69584
69504	69524	69541	69575	69585
69506	69526	69543	69576	69589
69512	69528	69545	69578	69592
69515	69529	69546	69579	69593
69517	69532	69549	69580	

Total 107

Often referred to as 'Top Shed' for the wealth of express classes shedded there, Kings Cross depot was the mecca for most spotters and enthusiasts. The shed began to decline in importance by 1959 insofar as steam was concerned as diesels were gradually introduced to the East coast main line.

At closure in June 1963 the engines were transferred to 34E New England and 34F Grantham. Demolition of the site was more or less complete by 1964.

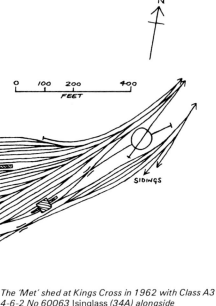

@1933

Kings Cross in 1956 as seen from the coaling tower. The locos in the centre are (left) 'A1' 60141 Abbotsford and 'V2' 60903. BR

The 'Met' shed at Kings Cross in 1962 with Class A3 4-6-2 No 60063 Isinglass (34A) alongside unidentified 'Deltic' and 'A4' locos. This part of the depot had, by this time, ceased playing host to the bulk of tank locos once shedded there. K. Fairey

34B HORNSEY

Pre-Grouping Origin: Great Northern Railway
Gazetteer Ref: 40 A5
Closed: 1961
Shed-Code: 34B (1949 to 1961)
Allocations: 1950

Class J6 0-6-0

64188	64234	64239	64251	64256

Class C12 4-4-2T

67376

Class J52 0-6-0ST

68757	68776	68787	68808	68833
68758	68777	68788	68811	68834
68759	68778	68791	68815	68851
68760	68781	68793	68825	68853
68761	68783	68794	68826	68856
68773	68784	68795	68827	68883
68774	68785	68796	68829	

Class N1 0-6-2T

69431	69441	69455	69463	69470
69432	69442	69456	69465	69475
69433	69445	69457	69466	69476
69434	69450	69458	69467	69477
69435	69451	69460	69468	69480
69439	69453	69462	69469	69481

Class N2 0-6-2T

69505	69522	69533	69566
69513	69530	69547	69567
69516	69531	69556	

Total 81

Allocations: 1959

Class J6 0-6-0

64196	64223	64233	64253	64266

Class J94 0-6-0ST

68033	68067	68073	68075	68077

Class J50 0-6-0T

68891	68920	68936	68971	68985
68894	68921	68945	68972	68986
68903	68926	68960	68979	68987
68906	68928	68961	68980	68989
68907	68929	68966	68981	68990
68917	68930	68968	68982	68991
68918	68931	68970	68983	

Class N2 0-6-2T

69505	69530	69556	69567	69594
69513	69533	69560	69572	
69522	69537	69561	69587	

Class WD 2-8-0

90454

Total 58

From the two sets of allocations one can see that the 'J52s' were replaced completely with the younger 'J50s' by 1959 as the former class went to the scrapheap in that decade. From a once numerous class only two remained by 1960 and both were allocated to the North Eastern Region.

Closure came in July 1961 and the bulk of the stud was moved to 34A Kings Cross, 34E New England and 36A Doncaster.

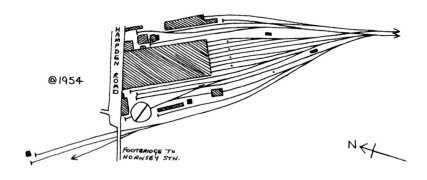

@1954

FOOTBRIDGE TO HORNSEY STN.

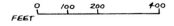

FEET

Hornsey shed in 1960 showing four Class J50 locos in the centre of the view. K. Fairey

A northerly view of Hornsey depot in 1957. W. Potter

34C HATFIELD

Pre-Grouping Origin: Great Northern Railway
Gazetteer Ref: 11 F2
Closed: 1961
Shed-Code: 34C (1949 to 1961)
Allocations: 1950

Classes J67* and J69 0-6-0T
68565   68572*

Class N1 0-6-2T
69484

Class N2 0-6-2T

69493	69534	69554	69580	69587
69494	69537	69558	69582	69588
69504	69551	69559	69586	69594

Class N7 0-6-2T

69613	69620	69639	69644	69695
69615	69632	69640	69691	69696

Total 28

Allocations: 1959

Class N2 0-6-2T

69531	69571	69582	69588
69547	69577	69586	69591

Class N7 0-6-2T

69618	69632	69648	69654	69704
69629	69638	69649	69692	
69631	69640	69650	69698	

Total 21

At closure in January 1961 the locos moved to 34A Kings Cross.

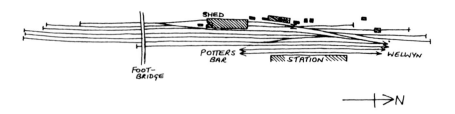

@1960

SHED

POTTERS BAR

STATION

WELLWYN

FOOT-BRIDGE

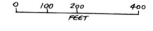

0   100   200   400
FEET

→ ▷N

50

A view of the south end of Hatfield depot taken in 1959 from the footbridge. C. I. K. Field

Class N2 No 69531 outside the shed at Hatfield in 1960. K. Fairey

34D HITCHIN

Pre-Grouping Origin: Great Northern Railway
Gazetteer Ref: 11 E2
Closed: 1961
Shed-Code: 34D (1949 to 1961)
Allocations: 1950

Class B1 4-6-0
61090   61093   61095   61099
61091   61094   61097   61105

Class J3 0-6-0
64105   64117   64140
64114   64122   64153

Class J6 0-6-0
64175   64240

Class J1 0-6-0
65003   65010   65013

Class L1 2-6-4T
67740   67743   67745   67790
67741   67744   67746   67791

Class Y3 0-4-0T
68175

Classes J67* and J69 0-6-0T
68512*   68541   68605

Class N2 0-6-2T
69515   69557

Total 33

Allocations: 1959

Class B1 4-6-0
61027 *Madoqua*   61094
61090   61097
61091   61139
61093   61251 *Oliver Bury*

Class J6 0-6-0
64175   64197   64237   64251
64184   64206   64240

Class J15 0-6-0
65479

Class L1 2-6-4T
67741   67745   67749   67785   67791
67744   67746   67761   67790

Class J68 0-6-0T
68661

Class N2 0-6-2T
69536   69540   69548

Total 29

Hitchin lost its allocation in 1960 but did not close to steam until June 1961 as it managed with engines on loan from New England up to closure.

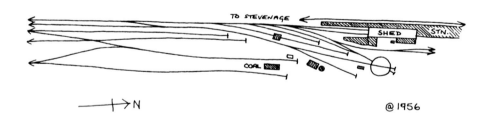

—⊢→N

@ 1956

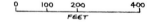

0   100   200   400
FEET

Two of Hitchin's 'B1s' outside the shed in 1955,
Nos 61094 and 61027 Madoqua. The station
platform alongside the shed-yard provided spotters
with a perfect vantage point to observe the daily
workings of the depot.   F. Dean

This view of two years later portrays Class L1 2-6-4T
No 67746 alongside the Hitchen shed office, with
'B1' 4-6-0 No 61097 occupying the other road (both
34D).   H. I. Cameron

34E NEASDEN

Pre-Grouping Origin: Great Central Railway
Gazetteer Ref: 39 B3
Closed: 1962
Shed-Codes: 34E (1949 to 1958)
14D (1958 to 1962)
Allocations: 1950 (34E)

Class 14xx 0-4-2T
1426

Class 61xx 2-6-2T
6129   6166

Class A3 4-6-2
60050 *Persimmon*
60051 *Blink Bonny*
60111 *Enterprise*

Class B1 4-6-0
61028 *Umseke*   61083   61163
61077   61140   61164

Class J11 0-6-0
64313   64329   64394

Class C13 4-4-2T
67418   67420

Class L1 2-6-4T
67707   67749   67761   67773   67782
67714   67751   67762   67774   67783
67715   67752   67767   67775   67784
67717   67753   67768   67776   67785
67718   67756   67769   67778   67786
67720   67757   67770   67779
67747   67758   67771   67780
67748   67760   67772   67781

Class Y3 0-4-0T
68172

Class L3 2-6-4T
69055   69060   69065
69056   69061   69067

Class N5 0-6-2T
69257   69300   69318   69358
69259   69302   69341   69369
69283   69315   69350

Class N7 0-6-2T
69689   69690   69692   69694   69698

Class A5 4-6-2T
69805   69822   69827   69828   69829

Total 82

Allocations: 1959 (14D)

Class 14xx 0-4-2T
1473

Class 54xx 0-6-0PT
5409

Class 2 2-6-2T
41270   41272   41284   41329

Class 4 2-6-4T
42157   42248   42256   42291   42588
42222   42249   42279   42437   42595
42225   42250   42281   42450   42618
42230   42251   42282   42453   42629
42231   42252   42283   42556
42232   42253   42284   42568

Class 5 4-6-0
44691   44830   45006   45260
44819   44847   45215   45416

Class B1 4-6-0
61077   61116   61136   61187   61206

Class N5 0-6-2T
69257   69319   69341

Class 4 2-6-0
76035   76037   76039   76041   76043
76036   76038   76040   76042   76044

Class 4 2-6-4T
80059   80137   80139   80141   80143
80083   80138   80140   80142   80144

Total 70

The motive power reorganisation of 1958 placed Neasden under the control of the London Midland Region which allocated the code 14D within the Cricklewood group of depots.

Perhaps the most cosmopolitan of all sheds, visitors were often treated to the sight of engines from no fewer than five regions under the one roof.

Upon closure in 1962 (whilst still in LMR control), the engines and men were transferred to 14A Cricklewood.

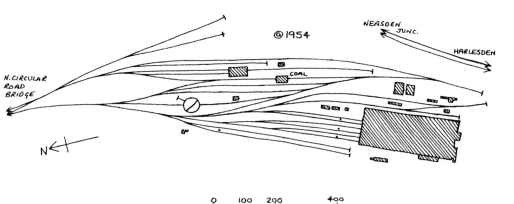

@1954

NEASDEN JUNC.

HARLESDEN

N. CIRCULAR ROAD BRIDGE

COAL

N

0   100   200   400
            FEET

Class D10 'Director' No 5430 Purdon Viccars
*outside Neasden shed in 1925. This loco survived
into the early 1950s and became BR No 62651.*
H. C. Casserley

*An overall view of Neasden in 1959 looking south
towards a group of Class 4 tanks locos amid a 'B1'
4-6-0.* M. S. Houlgrave

35A NEW ENGLAND

Pre-Grouping Origin: Great Northern Railway
Gazetteer Ref: 17F2
Closed: 1965
Shed-Codes: 35A (1949 to 1958)
34E (1958 to 1965)
Allocations: 1950 (35A)

Class A1 4-6-2
60113 *Great Northern*

Class A2 4-6-2
60500 *Edward Thompson*
60504 *Mons Meg*
60505 *Thane of Fife*
60506 *Wolf of Badenoch*
60508 *Duke of Rothesay*
60513 *Dante*
60514 *Chamossaire*
60520 *Owen Tudor*
60523 *Sun Castle*
60533 *Happy Knight*

Class V2 2-6-2

60803	60855	60871	60899	60916
60828	60858	60874	60905	60924
60829	60859	60876	60906	60936
60841	60863	60878	60908	60938
60842	60865	60879	60911	60950
60850	60866	60893	60912	60966
60854	60869	60897	60913	

Class B1 4-6-0
61027 *Madoqua*

61070	61075	61206	61210	61331
61073	61143	61207	61330	

Class K2 2-6-0

61729	61735	61739	61747
61730	61736	61740	

Classes K3 and K5* 2-6-0

61804	61850	61867	61929	61972
61811	61853	61868	61951	
61841	61862	61890	61954	
61843	61863*	61915	61967	

Class O2 2-8-0

63923	63933	63935	63948

Classes J3 and J4* 0-6-0

64112*	64121*	64131	64158
64118	64123	64135	64160*
64120*	64128	64151	64162*

Class J6 0-6-0

64171	64189	64217	64238	64257
64176	64191	64220	64245	64265
64177	64192	64221	64246	64266
64184	64207	64225	64249	64273
64186	64211	64228	64252	64275
64187	64216	64235	64254	64278

Class J1 0-6-0

65002	65004	65005	65006

Class C12 4-4-2T

67357	67365	67373
67361	67368	67390

Class Y1 0-4-0T
68133S

Class Y3 0-4-0T
68185

Class J66 0-6-0T
68387

Class J69 0-6-0T
68632

Class J52 0-6-0ST

68765	68819	68824	68850	68876
68789	68820	68840	68852	68879
68798	68821	68844	68866	68880
68817	68823	68846	68868	

Class L3 2-6-4T
69064

Class N5 0-6-2T
69337

Class WD 2-8-0

90028	90106	90244	90438	90554
90031	90130	90253	90439	90559
90034	90151	90256	90447	90577
90059	90156	90259	90454	90613
90062	90158	90279	90490	90657
90063	90165	90287	90494	90659
90070	90169	90288	90495	90665
90079	90180	90305	90501	90683
90088	90191	90346	90512	90730
90093	90208	90349	90514	
90096	90239	90428	90528	

Total 213

Allocations: 1959 (34E)

Class 4 2-6-0

43067	43082	43086
43081	43084	43088

Class A2 4-6-2
60500 *Edward Thompson*   60508 *Duke of Rothesay*
60504 *Mons Meg*   60514 *Chamossaire*
60505 *Thane of Fife*   60523 *Sun Castle*
60506 *Wolf of Badenoch*

Class V2 2-6-2

60821	60845	60869	60897	60924
60826	60850	60874	60906	60966
60829	60853	60875	60908	
60832	60867	60893	60912	

Class B1 4-6-0

61060	61073	61113	61210	61302
61070	61074	61207	61282	61391

Class K2 2-6-0

61759	61777

Class K3 2-6-0
| 61805 | 61830 | 61864 | 61978 | 61979 |

Class J6 0-6-0
| 64177 | 64224 | 64254 | 64272 |
| 64210 | 64228 | 64265 | 64279 |

Class J50 0-6-0T
| 68896 | 68976 |

Class N5 0-6-2T
| 69262 | 69267 | 69276 | 69293 |
| 69266 | 69274 | 69292 | 69327 |

Class WD 2-8-0
90000	90158	90223	90269	90613
90015	90165	90239	90349	90659
90096	90169	90246	90428	90665
90151	90180	90253	90439	90730

Class 9F 2-10-0
92036	92042	92143	92148	92181
92037	92044	92144	92149	92182
92038	92140	92145	92178	92183
92040	92141	92146	92179	92187
92041	92142	92147	92180	92188

Total 111

Upon closure in January 1965, most of the locos transferred to 40E Colwick and 41J Langwith, but many went for scrap.
In 1952/3 the shed was rebuilt.

New England shed in 1957 looking north. An unusual feature of the south end of the shed was the overhead gantry which carried the loco water supply to each of the nine tracks and part of it can be seen here. BR

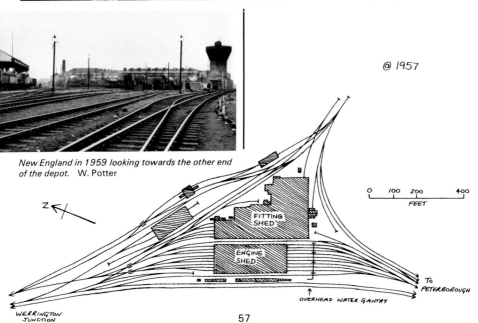

New England in 1959 looking towards the other end of the depot. W. Potter

@ 1957

FITTING SHED

ENGINE SHED

To PETERBOROUGH

↑
OVERHEAD WATER GANTRY

WERRINGTON JUNCTION

0   100   200   400
FEET

35B GRANTHAM

Pre-Grouping Origin: Great Northern Railway
Gazetteer Ref: 16 D1
Closed: 1963
Shed-Codes: 35B (1949 to 1958)
34F (1958 to 1963)
Allocations: 1950 (35B)

Class A4 4-6-2
60015 *Quicksilver*
60026 *Miles Beevor*

Class A3 4-6-2
60053 *Sansovino*
60106 *Flying Fox*

Class B12 4-6-0
61538   61541   61553   61554   61565

Class D3 4-4-0
62000

Class C1 4-4-2
62822

Class O2 2-8-0
63929   63932   63940   63960
63930   63936   63949   63965
63931   63938   63950   63966

Class J6 0-6-0
64172   64178   64206   64227   64237

Class C12 4-4-2T
67380   67382

Class J52 0-6-0ST
68801   68877

Class A5 4-6-2T
69803   69816   69824

Total 35

*Of the two buildings at Grantham, this, the 'new'
shed is shown in 1963 with a 'WD' class loco
simmering outside.* K. Fairey

Allocations: 1959 (34F)

Class A3 4-6-2
60047 *Donovan*   60063 *Isinglass*
60048 *Doncaster*   60065 *Knight of Thistle*
60049 *Galtee More*   60105 *Victor Wild*
60050 *Persimmon*   60106 *Flying Fox*
60054 *Prince of Wales* 60107 *Royal Lancer*
60056 *Centenary*   60111 *Enterprise*

Class A2 4-6-2
60513 *Dante*
60520 *Owen Tudor*
60533 *Happy Knight*

Class B1 4-6-0
61389   61392

Class O2 2-8-0
63923   63931   63936   63946   63960
63929   63932   63938   63948   63966
63930   63933   63940   63950

Class J6 0-6-0
64181   64192   64246

Class L1 2-6-4T
67794

Class J69 0-6-0T
68626   68635

Class N2 0-6-2T
69516   69552

Class A5 4-6-2T
69814   69827

Total 41

In 1951 a triangle of trackage was constructed to
replace the two turntables previously used.
  Upon closure in 1963, most of the remaining
serviceable stock was reallocated to Doncaster
(36A).

58

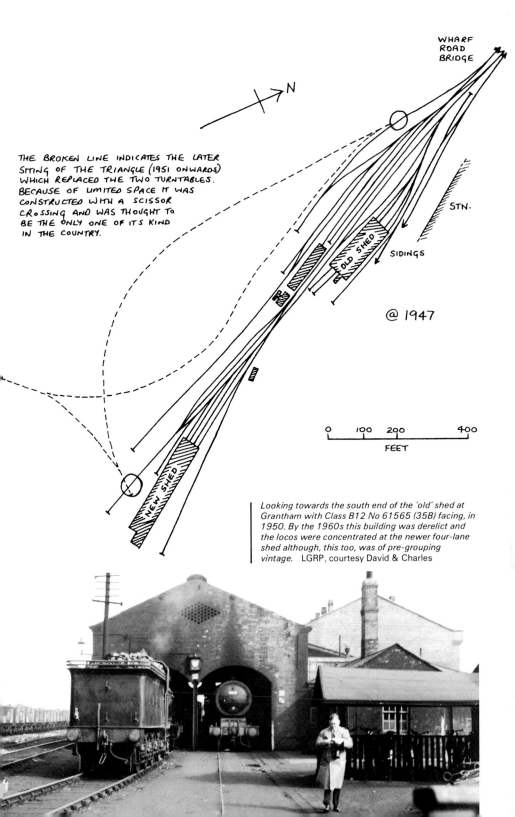

N

THE BROKEN LINE INDICATES THE LATER
SITING OF THE TRIANGLE (1951 ONWARDS)
WHICH REPLACED THE TWO TURNTABLES.
BECAUSE OF LIMITED SPACE IT WAS
CONSTRUCTED WITH A SCISSOR
CROSSING AND WAS THOUGHT TO
BE THE ONLY ONE OF ITS KIND
IN THE COUNTRY.

WHARF
ROAD
BRIDGE

STN.

SIDINGS

OLD SHED

@ 1947

NEW SHED

0   100   200   400
FEET

Looking towards the south end of the 'old' shed at
Grantham with Class B12 No 61565 (35B) facing, in
1950. By the 1960s this building was derelict and
the locos were concentrated at the newer four-lane
shed although, this too, was of pre-grouping
vintage. LGRP, courtesy David & Charles

35C PETERBOROUGH SPITAL BRIDGE

Being of Midland Railway origin and not transferring to the Eastern Region until 1950, this depot has been catered for in the LMR volume under its previous code 16B.

36A DONCASTER

Pre-Grouping Origin: Great Northern Railway
Gazetteer Ref: 21 F5
Closed: 1966
Shed-Code: 36A (1949 to 1966)
Allocations: 1950

Class A3 4-6-2
60047 *Donovan*
60055 *Woolwinder*
60058 *Blair Atholl*
60061 *Pretty Polly*
60064 *Tagalie*
60066 *Merry Hampton*

Class V2 2-6-2

60846	60889
60849	60890
60852	60896
60857	60902
60861	60917
60867	60921
60870	60928
60872 *Kings Own Yorkshire Light Infantry*	60930
60875	60935
60877	60943
60880	60948
60881	60956

Class B1 4-6-0
61026 *Ourebi*
61036 *Ralph Assheton*
61086
61087
61107
61120
61124
61125
61126
61127
61128
61170
61193
61196
61246 *Lord Balfour of Burleigh*
61247 *Lord Burghley*
61248 *Geoffrey Gibbs*
61249 *Fitzherbert Wright*
61250 *A. Harold Bibby*
61265

Class K3 2-6-0

61861	61907	61918	61978

Class O3 2-8-0

63476	63479	63483	63486	63493
63477	63480	63484	63488	
63478	63481	63485	63491	

Class O2 2-8-0

63925	63945	63954	63961	63974
63926	63946	63955	63962	63986
63928	63947	63956	63964	63987
63941	63951	63957	63967	
63942	63952	63958	63968	
63943	63953	63959	63973	

Class J3 0-6-0
64124

Class J6 0-6-0

64179	64195	64232	64258	64263
64183	64209	64236	64259	64264
64185	64218	64243	64261	64270
64193	64219	64255	64262	64279

Class J11 0-6-0

64285	64349	64410

Class J39 0-6-0

64713	64835	64902	64952	64984
64721	64885	64909	64967	
64737	64891	64910	64976	
64758	64893	64951	64977	

Class J21 0-6-0

65095	65117

Class Y1 0-4-0T
68132S

Class Y3 0-4-0T
68165S

Class J55 0-6-0ST
68319S

Class J52 0-6-0ST

68763	68804	68841	68858	68885
68769	68806	68842	68860	68886
68775	68813	68843	68865	
68782S	68835	68847	68867	
68786	68836	68849	68869	
68800	68837	68857	68870	

Class J50 0-6-0T

68893	68926	68961	68986	68991
68917	68936	68980	68987	
68918	68945	68985	68989	

Class J72 0-6-0T
69014

Total 180

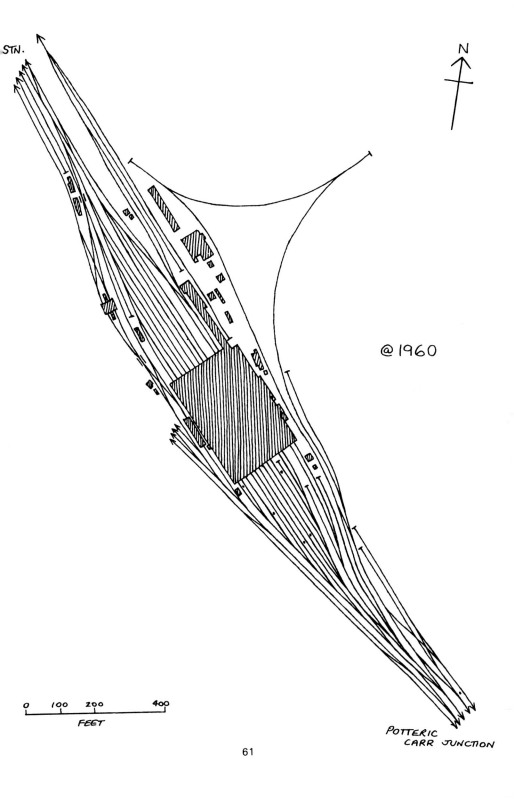

STN.

N

@1960

0   100   200   400
FEET

POTTERIC
CARR JUNCTION

61

Allocations: 1959

Class A3 4-6-2

60046 *Diamond Jubilee*	60104 *Solario*
60064 *Tagalie*	60108 *Gay Crusader*
60067 *Ladas*	60112 *St Simon*
60102 *Sir Frederick Banbury*	

Class A1 4-6-2

60113 *Great Northern*	60139 *Sea Eagle*
60114 *W. P. Allen*	60144 *King's Courier*
60119 *Patrick Stirling*	60149 *Amadis*
60122 *Curlew*	60156 *Great Central*
60125 *Scottish Union*	60157 *Great Eastern*
60128 *Bongrace*	60158 *Aberdonian*
60136 *Alcazar*	

Class W1 4-6-4
60700

Class V2 2-6-2

60817	60899
60841	60905
60849	60909
60852	60917
60857	60921
60866	60928
60870	60930
60872 *Kings Own Yorkshire Light Infantry*	60935
60880	60936
60881	60943
60889	60956
60896	

Class B1 4-6-0

61036 *Ralph Assheton*	61158
61087	61170
61107	61193
61114	61196
61120	61213
61121	61225
61122	61247 *Lord Burghley*
61124	61250 *A. Harold Bibby*
61125	61266
61127	61285
61128	61326
61145	61365
61155	61377
61157	

Class K3 2-6-0

61800	61812	61887	61925	61961
61803	61829	61895	61940	61964

Class O4 2-8-0

63613	63677	63698
63618	63693	63858

Class O2 2-8-0

63922	63943	63957	63969	63983
63928	63951	63958	63973	63984
63934	63952	63962	63974	63985
63935	63953	63963	63975	
63939	63954	63964	63977	
63941	63955	63967	63978	
63942	63956	63968	63981	

Class J6 0-6-0

64179	64209	64241	64259
64185	64232	64258	64270

Class J39 0-6-0

64716	64737	64874	64909	64987
64721	64810	64876	64967	
64722	64827	64883	64972	
64723	64838	64885	64981	

Class J94 0-6-0ST

68020	68022	68069	68071

Class J69 0-6-0T

68498	68508	68556	68587
68502	68520	68558	68621
68507	68530	68569	

Class J68 0-6-0T
68654

Class J50 0-6-0T

68962	68964	68965	68973

Class WD 2-8-0

90108	90453	90550	90636
90144	90537	90569	90696
90255	90538	90602	90732 *Vulcan*

Class 9F 2-10-0

92168	92172	92176	92192
92169	92173	92177	92199
92170	92174	92189	92200
92171	92175	92191	92201

Total 191

Allocations: 1965

Class B1 4-6-0
61039 *Steinbok*

61051	61121	61196	61329
61087	61157	61225	61360
61093	61158	61326	61367

Class O4 2-8-0

63593	63730	63818
63613	63764	63858

Class WD 2-8-0

90001	90195	90296	90476	90569
90018	90235	90305	90477	90580
90063	90252	90365	90480	90636
90073	90255	90369	90484	90675
90096	90277	90372	90498	90683
90154	90279	90421	90506	90687
90156	90293	90428	90538	90709

Class 9F 2-10-0

92168	92173	92183	92190	92201
92172	92174	92186	92200	

Total 63

Closing in April 1966, Doncaster was the last steam shed on the Eastern Region. All its steam locos went for scrapping but the depot retained its facilities for the odd visitor from the North Eastern Region.

The south-eastern end of Doncaster shed in 1963 with Classes A3, B1, 9F, A1 and V2 on display. K. Fairey

Looking towards the north-western end of Doncaster in 1950 showing the huge coaler on the right. LGRP, courtesy David & Charles

36B MEXBOROUGH

Pre-Grouping Origin: Great Central Railway
Gazetteer Ref: 21 F4
Closed: 1964
Shed-Codes: 36B (1949 to 1958)
41F (1958 to 1964)
Allocations: 1950 (36B)

Class B1 4-6-0

61165	61167	61174
61166	61168	61194

Class 04 2-8-0

63611	63668	63774	63791
63612	63672	63775	63813
63627	63682	63779	63898

Class 02 2-8-0

63924	63971	63977	63981	63985
63927	63972	63978	63982	
63969	63975	63979	63983	
63970	63976	63980	63984	

Class J11 0-6-0

64283	64319	64374	64404
64288	64334	64377	64432
64296	64352	64400	64442
64302	64356	64403	64449

Class J50 0-6-0T

68890	68946	68960	68974

Class N5 0-6-2T

69264	69297	69314	69316

Class S1 0-8-4T

69900	69901	69904	69905

Class WD 2-8-0

90104	90195	90270	90410	90598
90108	90196	90280	90421	90612
90120	90209	90285	90521	90618
90144	90211	90286	90537	90653
90146	90220	90290	90538	90696
90150	90223	90296	90550	90700
90153	90229	90301	90583	90709
90154	90232	90311	90587	90714
90161	90246	90340	90590	
90166	90250	90383	90594	
90189	90252	90400	90596	
90190	90255	90401	90597	

Total 119

Allocations: 1959 (41F)

Class B1 4-6-0

61112	61165	61166	61167	61194

Class K3 2-6-0

61836	61839	61850	61867	61868

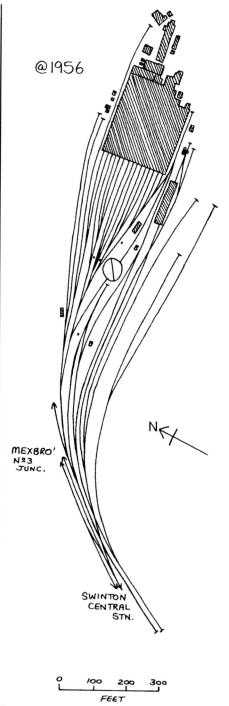

@1956

N

MEXBRO'
Nº3
JUNC.

SWINTON
CENTRAL
STN.

```
0      100    200    300
|_____|
        FEET
```

Class 04 2-8-0				
63586	63673	63756	63798	63843
63593	63684	63757	63812	63891
63611	63701	63764	63813	63894
63628	63723	63774	63828	63897
63666	63730	63779	63832	83898
63672	63753	63791	63841	63908

Class J11 0-6-0

64377	64393	64402	64406

Class J69 0-6-0T

68497	68623

Class N5 0-6-2T

69308

Class WD 2-8-0				
90119	90211	90304	90421	90580
90136	90220	90311	90491	90582
90139	90250	90330	90495	90587
90153	90252	90358	90499	90590
90190	90270	90384	90506	90608
90195	90286	90400	90521	90612
90203	90290	90401	90526	90668
90209	90301	90410	90567	90700

Total 87

At closure most of the remaining locos went to Staveley Barrow Hill (41E) and Canklow (41D). Both these depots transferred to the Eastern Region in 1958 from the London Midland Region and are catered for in the latter volume because of their Midland Railway origins.

Mexborough shed in 1958 clearly showing a predominance of freight classes over passenger.
W. Potter

Another view of Mexborough taken the same day from a different angle.   W. Potter

36C FRODINGHAM

Pre-Grouping Origin: Great Central Railway
Gazetteer Ref: 22 F4
Closed: 1966
Shed-Code: 36C (1949 to 1966)
Allocations: 1950

Class 04 2-8-0

63572	63626	63660	63731	63832
63576	63640	63669	63744	63847
63584	63642	63671	63745	63906
63587	63643	63684	63747	63911
63595	63645	63690	63778	63917
63601	63649	63696	63788	63920
63602	63653	63718	63793	
63606	63655	63726	63818	
63617	63659	63728	63824	

Class 02 2-8-0

63922	63937	63944
63934	63939	63963

Class J11 0-6-0

64308	64339	64407
64309	64395	64429

Class J50 0-6-0T

68962	68968	68971	68979
68964	68970	68973	

Class L3 2-6-4T
69051

Class S1 0-8-4T

69902	69903

Class Q1 0-8-0T

69930	69934	69936
69932	69935	69937

Total 70

Allocations: 1959

Class 04 2-8-0

63572	63626	63671	63747	63807
63576	63642	63690	63761	63880
63595	63653	63696	63781	63906
63601	63654	63728	63788	63917
63606	63660	63741	63793	
63617	63662	63744	63799	

Class J11 0-6-0

64308	64319	64365	64429
64315	64351	64407	

Class J50 0-6-0T

68963	68977

Class Q1 0-8-0T

69928	69939	69934	69935	69936

Class WD 2-8-0

90013	90111	90456	90597	90714
90031	90133	90469	90598	
90032	90232	90490	90601	
90059	90422	90512	90646	
90070	90425	90540	90647	

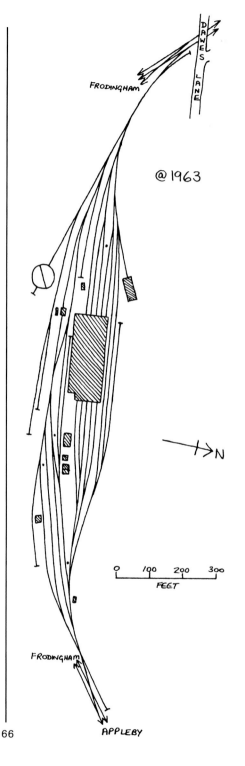

@ 1963

Class 9F 2-10-0

92034	92184	92190	92198
92035	92185	92197	

Total 70

Allocations: 1965

Class K1 2-6-0

62014	62015	62017	62035	62067

Class 04 2-8-0

63586	63628	63671	63788	63793
63606	63653	63781	63791	

Class WD 2-8-0

90000	90053	90248	90439	90601
90007	90108	90274	90456	90613
90013	90115	90283	90493	90665
90024	90133	90315	90516	
90025	90166	90381	90537	
90032	90232	90422	90540	

Total 41

Frodingham was one of the last depots on the Eastern Region to have a steam allocation, albeit a relatively uninteresting one in the form of freight classes only. One possible distinction was that it played host to the last five Class Q1 locos in 1959 before they went for scrap in the same year. Upon closure in February 1966, the few remaining WD locos went to 36A Doncaster.

Three Class 04 engines, Nos 63628, 63601 and 63781 (all 36C) are pictured here at the western end of Frodingham depot in 1963. K. Fairey

An overall view of the western end of Frodingham shed in 1950 with many different types on display.
LGRP, courtesy David & Charles

36D BARNSLEY

Pre-Grouping Origin: Great Central Railway
Gazetteer Ref: 42 E2
Closed: 1960
Shed-Codes: 36D (1949 to 1958)
41G (1958 to 1960)
Allocations: 1950 (36D)

Class Q4 0-8-0
63201	63203	63220	63229	63235

Class O4 2-8-0
63623	63727	63904
63697	63883	63913

Class J11 0-6-0
64290	64366	64399	64448
64343	64391	64425	64452
64362	64398	64436	

Class C13 4-4-2T
67409	67411	67434

Class N5 0-6-2T
69268	69291	69325	69348	69365
69278	69303	69334	69355	69367
69285	69320	69345	69357	69368

Total 40

Allocations: 1959 (41G)

Class O4 2-8-0
63612	63669	63726	63802	63904
63623	63697	63727	63824	63907
63656	63704	63731	63836	63911
63659	63718	63763	63883	63913

Class J11 0-6-0
64376	64404	64425	64452
64403	64417	64442	

Class J39 0-6-0
64828
64902

Class C14 4-4-2T
67445	67448

Class N5 0-6-2T
69268	69342	69354
69320	69343	69370

Total 37

Upon closure the engines and men were transferred to Mexborough 41F. The shed buildings were demolished in the year of closure.

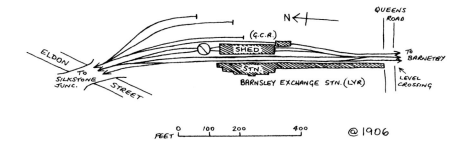

BARNSLEY EXCHANGE STN. (LYR)

@ 1906

Barnsley in 1954 from the Queens Road level crossing. Despite the small two lane shed, no fewer than 41 locos were 'on shed' this day. As will be seen in the diagram, there were no sidings near to the crossing in 1906 and it is likely that these were added in LNER days. Locos were also stored in sidings either side of the main line south of this crossing.   B. Hilton

Looking towards Barnsley shed with its rebuilt roof in 1957. Class C14 4-4-2T No 67434 (36D) is one of the three locos in line on the right.   W. Potter

36E RETFORD

Pre-Grouping Origin: Great Northern Railway and Great Central Railway*
Gazetteer Ref: 16 A3
Closed: 1965*
Shed-Code: 36E (1949 to 1965)
Allocations: 1950

Class B1 4-6-0
61208	61211	61212	61213	61231

Class O3 2-8-0
63475	63482

Class O4 2-8-0
63608	63688	63782	63905	63914
63637	63736	63785	63907	
63654	63763	63877	63908	

Class J3 0-6-0
64125	64133	64141	64148	64150

Class J6 0-6-0
64241

Class J11 0-6-0
64280	64306	64347	64393	64421
64282	64335	64348	64402	64422
64287	64340	64380	64413	64423
64295	64341	64385	64416	64451

Class J39 0-6-0
64759	64898	64908	64961	64987
64830	64906	64956	64970	

Class J21 0-6-0
65070

Class J52 0-6-0ST
68766

Class N5 0-6-2T
69273	69282	69313	69354
69277	69294	69321	

Total 64

Allocations: 1959

Class B1 4-6-0
61126	61208	61211	61212	61231

Class O4 2-8-0
63608	63655	63736	63785	63914
63637	63688	63782	63818	

Class O2 2-8-0
63924	63944	63961	63976	63987
63925	63945	63965	63979	
63926	63947	63970	63980	
63927	63949	63971	63982	
63937	63959	63972	63986	

Class J6 0-6-0
64174	64188	64236
64178	64234	64245

Class J11 0-6-0
64280	64287	64385	64421	64450
64283	64321	64395	64423	64451

Class J39 0-6-0
64714	64830	64893	64906	64970
64759	64882	64898	64908	

Class N5 0-6-2T
69322

Total 61

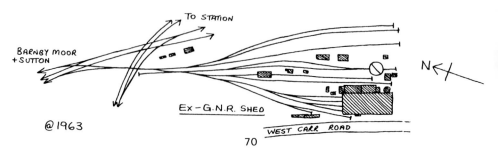

THE TWO SHEDS WERE CONSIDERED '36E' AND ARE THUS BOTH PORTRAYED. THEY WERE APPROX. 700 YARDS APART.

0 100 200 400
FEET

Ex - G.C.R. SHED

F.B.

TO STATION

WORKS

WORKS

@ 1963

N

TO CLARBOROUGH TUNNEL

LONDON ROAD (A.I.)

BARNBY MOOR + SUTTON

TO STATION

Ex - G.N.R. SHED

WEST CARR ROAD

@ 1963

N

Allocations: 1965

Class B1 4-6-0

61050	61058	61127	61348
61055	61107	61208	61384

Class 04 2-8-0

63607	63661	63734	63785
63651	63688	63738	

Class WD 2-8-0

90130	90223	90454	90522	90557
90146	90280	90460	90528	90669
90158	90285	90501	90533	90689
90169	90349	90514	90551	90718

Total 35

* Retford consisted of two buildings, one of Great Central origin the other Great Northern and were considered one depot. The GCR portion was closed in January 1965 and demolished soon after to clear the way for construction of the Retford flyunder. The GNR shed soldiered on until June amid very cramped conditions as a result of the concentration of locos which were reported as being in a bad state of repair. At complete closure those engines still fit for use were transferred to Doncaster, Frodingham and Colwick.

Retford GNR in 1950 with Class JII 0-6-0 No 64393 (36E) nearest the camera.
LGRP, courtesy David & Charles

The rebuilt GNR shed at Retford in April 1965, a few months before closure. K. Fairey

Looking east to the GCR building at Retford from the footbridge in 1957. B. Hilton

An overall view of Retford GCRs sidings in 1963 with a good deal of the allocation lying silent on the metals. The eastern end of the shed is visible beyond the right of the sheer-legs. K. Fairey

37A ARDSLEY

Pre-Grouping Origin: Great Northern Railway
Gazetteer Ref: 42 B3
Closed: 1965
Shed-Codes: 37A (1949 to 1956)
56B (1956 to 1965)
Allocations: 1950 (37A)

Class B1 4-6-0
61029 *Chamois*
61031 *Reedbuck*
61033 *Dibatag*
61085
61096
61297
61309
61310

Class B4 4-6-0
61482 *Immingham*

Class Q4 0-8-0

63202	63217	63225	63234	63243
63204	63221	63226	63236	
63205	63223	63227	63240	

Class J3 0-6-0

64116	64119	64129	64142

Class J6 0-6-0

64174	64208	64267	64277
64182	64214	64272	

Class J39 0-6-0

64749	64796	64811	64840	64911
64751	64799	64825	64872	64979
64754	64801	64836	64896	64985
64760	64806	64839	64907	

Class C12 4-4-2T
67386

Class C14 4-4-2T

67440	67443	67445	67451
67441	67444	67446	

Class J52 0-6-0ST

68790	68848	68871	68872

Class J50 0-6-0T

68896	68907	68916	68938	68951
68900	68909	68919	68939	68966
68901	68910	68921	68947	
68903	68914	68930	68948	
68904	68915	68931	68949	

Class N1 0-6-2T

69452	69461

Total 88

@ 1951

To WAKEFIELD

N

0   100   200   400
FEET

WALLS

FALL
LANE

To STN.

Ardsley in 1957 under North Eastern Region control.
This easterly view is that which was obtained from
the Fall Lane overbridge. K. Fairey

Allocations: 1959 (56B)				

Class 4 2-6-0
43075   43101

Class 3F 0-6-0T
47443   47589   47632   47640

Class V2 2-6-2
60861   60884   60916

Class B1 4-6-0
61013 *Topi*   61123   61297
61110   61295   61310

Class 04 2-8-0
63570   63605   63724   63885
63584   63633   63823

Class J6 0-6-0
64182   64208   64222   64268

Class J39 0-6-0
64705   64757   64825   64839   64979
64720   64760   64831   64840
64732   64806   64833   64879
64749   64811   64836   64918
64754   64820   64837   64969

Class J52 0-6-0ST
68824   68834   68869   68875

Class J50 0-6-0T
68890   68902   68916   68937
68900   68914   68919   68938
68901   68915   68935   68947

Total 63

Allocations: 1965 (56B)

Class 4MT 2-6-0
43070   43101   43137
43096   43132   43141

Class A1 4-6-2
60117 *Bois Roussel*   60133 *Pommern*
60130 *Kestrel*   60148 *Aboyeur*

Class V2 2-6-2
60843   60923

Class B1 4-6-0
61013 *Topi*   61238 *Leslie Runciman*
61014 *Oribi*   61240 *Harry Hinchcliffe*
61016 *Inyala*   61259
61017 *Bushbuck*   61291
61030 *Nyala*   61304
61061   61322
61110   61385
61218   61388
61237 *Geoffrey H. Kitson*

Class WD 2-8-0
90047   90230   90405   90625
90056   90236   90409   90642
90126   90240   90465   90644
90135   90361   90481   90731

Total 45

The shed became North Eastern Region property in 1956 taking up the new code of 56B.

Upon closure, still as 56B, in late 1965, the remaining engines were reallocated to at least eight other North Eastern depots.

Classes J6 0-6-0 and V2 2-6-2 Nos 64222 and 60916 (both 56B) at the south-east end of Ardsley depot in 1959. K. Fairey

37B COPLEY HILL

Pre-Grouping Origin: Great Northern Railway
Gazetteer Ref: 42 A3
Closed: 1964
Shed-Codes: 37B (1949 to 1956)
56C (1956 to 1964)
Allocations: 1950 (37B)

Class A3 4-6-2
60044 *Melton*   60062 *Minoru*
60046 *Diamond Jubilee* 60112 *St Simon*
60056 *Centenary*

Class A1 4-6-2
60114 *W. P. Allan*   60123 *H. A. Ivatt*
60117 *Bois Roussel*   60125 *Scottish Union*
60118 *Archibald Sturrock* 60133 *Pommern*
60119 *Patrick Stirling*   60134 *Foxhunter*
60120 *Kittiwake*   60141 *Abbotsford*

Class B1 4-6-0
61295

Class J6 0-6-0
64173   64250   64260

Class C12 4-4-2T
67353   67372

Class J50 0-6-0T
68911   68925   68978   68988
68913   68937   68984

Class N5 0-6-2T
69266   69271

Class N1 0-6-2T
69430   69437   69444   69471   69473
69436   69440   69446   69472

                                   Total 39

Allocations: 1959 (56C)

Class 3 2-6-2T
40074   40112   40114   40190

Class A1 4-6-2
60117 *Bois Roussel*   60131 *Osprey*
60118 *Archibald Sturrock* 60133 *Pommern*
60120 *Kittiwake*   60134 *Foxhunter*
60123 *H. A. Ivatt*   60141 *Abbotsford*
60130 *Kestrel*   60148 *Aboyeur*

Class V2 2-6-2
60859   60885

Class B1 4-6-0
61115   61320
61129   61339
61189 *Sir William Gray* 61386
61214   61388
61309

Class J6 0-6-0
64173   64277

Class J39 0-6-0
64911

Class J50 0-6-0T
68911   68913   68925   68984   68988

                                   Total 33

Copley Hill transferred to the North Eastern Region in
1956 and upon closure in 1964 had its duties taken
over by Neville Hill 55H.

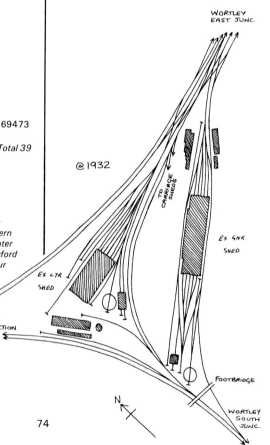

@ 1932

The ex-LYR shed, known as
'Wortley Junction'(closed 1928)
has also been included in view
of the close proximity of the
two buildings.

FEET 0 100 200 400

The south-west end of the through shed at Copley Hill in 1952 depicting 'V2' No 60826, 'J6' No 64277 and 'J50' No 68937 (all Copley Hill engines). The carriage shed is visible on the extreme left beyond which stood the single ended six road building (see map). N. E. Preedy

Class A3 4-6-2 No 60056 Centenary outside Copley Hill about 1960. This loco was allocated to Grantham 35B (later 34F) for most of its BR lifespan and was withdrawn in 1963. The smoke-deflectors carried were of German design (where fitted) and were not introduced until BR days. Eric Treacy

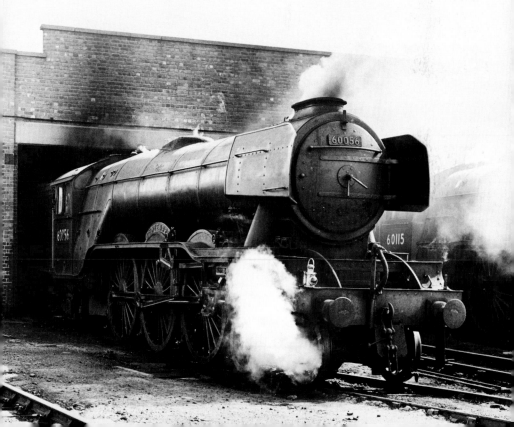

37C BRADFORD HAMMERTON STREET

Pre-Grouping Origin: Great Northern Railway
Gazetteer Ref: 42 B4
Closed: 1958
Shed-Codes: 37C (1949 to 1956)
56G (1956 to 1958)
Allocations: 1950 (37C)

Class B1 4-6-0

61229	61267	61294
61230	61268	61296

Class J6 0-6-0

64170	64205	64268	64274
64203	64226	64271	

Class C14 4-4-2T

67447	67448	67450

Class J50 0-6-0T

68892	68902	68922	68934	68943
68895	68906	68923	68940	68944
68897	68908	68932	68941	68959
68898	68912	68933	68942	68969

Class N1 0-6-2T

69443	49449	69464	69479	69485
69447	69454	69474	69482	
69448	69459	69478	69483	

Total 49

In 1954 part of the accommodation was set aside for the coming of diesel multiple units in the same year. When finally closing to steam in January 1958 the motive power was transferred to Low Moor 56F.

As was the case with Ardsley and Copley Hill depots, Hammerton Street was also transferred to the North Eastern Region's control in 1956, thus rendering the 37 group of sheds extinct within the Eastern Region.

The depot was sometimes referred to as 'Bowling Junction'.

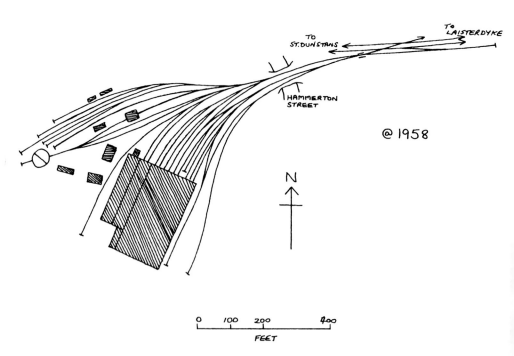

76

Hammerton Street in 1957 whilst under the control of the North Eastern Region. The engine illustrated is Class N1 No 69443 which formed part of the depot's allocation in that year.   K. Fairey

A different view of the same engine with the Hammenton Street's coaling plant in the background.   K. Fairey

77

38A COLWICK

Pre-Grouping Origin: Great Northern Railway
Gazetteer Ref: 41 F5
Closed: 1966
Shed-Codes: 38A (1949 to 1958)
40E (1958 to 1966)
16B (1966)
Allocations: 1950 (38A)

COLWICK
NORTH JUNCTION

@ 1952

COLWICK
SIDINGS

N

VICTORIA ROAD

Class B1 4-6-0

61078	61111	61123	61283	61368
61110	61122	61131	61367	61369

Class B17 4-6-0
61652 *Darlington*
61653 *Huddersfield Town*
61657 *Doncaster Rovers*
61662 *Manchester United*

Class K2 2-6-0

61723	61741	61758	61769
61726	61749	61763	61771
61732	61751	61768	61773

Class K3 2-6-0

61812	61821	61826
61816	61824	61833

Class D3 4-4-0
62148

Class D2 4-4-0
62172

Class O4 2-8-0

63573	63729	63761	63787	63829
63599	63735	63762	63801	63851
63636	63756	63781	63804	63894

Class J6 0-6-0

64194	64202	64222	64231
64197	64212	64223	64233
64199	64213	64224	64253
64200	64215	64230	64269

Class J11 0-6-0
64301

Class J39 0-6-0

64716	64739	64763	64831	64974
64719	64747	64805	64832	64980
64720	64750	64807	64837	64981
64729	64757	64827	64955	64983
64735	64762	64828	64965	64988

Class J1 0-6-0

65007	65008	65009	65014

0   100   200   400   FEET

SIDINGS

Class J2 0-6-0
65018   65019   65022   65023

Class J5 0-6-0
65480   65484   65488   65492   65498
65481   65485   65489   65493   65499
65482   65486   65490   65496
65483   65487   65491   65497

Class J52 0-6-0ST
68762   68779   68810   68839   68875
68767   68792   68812   68859   68882
68768   68807   68814   68863   68887

Class J50 0-6-0T
68891   68920   68972
68894   68935   68982

Class N5 0-6-2T
69312   69324

Class N2 0-6-2T
69501   69550   69552   69555

Class A5 4-6-2T
69801   69809   69817   69825
69806   69810   69821   69826
69807   69814   69823

Class WD 2-8-0
90000   90111   90330   90484   90636
90002   90129   90358   90491   90648
90025   90136   90368   90492   90662
90036   90139   90369   90499   90672
90043   90202   90391   90532   90676
90050   90215   90411   90544   90697
90073   90251   90437   90551   90703
90084   90303   90448   90574   90717
90103   90323   90466   90629

Total 199

Allocations: 1959 (40E)

Class 4 2-6-0
43154   43155   43158

Class B1 4-6-0
61088   61141   61177   61188   61281
61092   61163   61185   61209   61299

Class K2 2-6-0
61723   61752   61754
61738   61753   61780

Class K3 2-6-0
61808   61837   61873   61914   61982
61821   61852   61888   61947
61833   61870   61896   61974

Classes 01* and 04 2-8-0
63585   63602   63674   63768*   63873
63587   63614   63675   63770
63589*   63639   63694   63816
63592*   63647   63699   63859
63594*   63657   63754   63863*

Class J6 0-6-0
64213   64238   64257   64273
64235   64239   64269

Class J11 0-6-0
64348   64397   64438

Class J39 0-6-0
64712   64762   64832   64976   64983
64715   64763   64887   64977   64988
64735   64802   64974   64980

Class L1 2-6-4T
67753   67758   67760   67788   67799

Class J94 0-6-0ST
68028   68072   68076

Class J69 0-6-0T
68522   68545   68550   68601   68629

Class J50 0-6-0T
68893   68950   68974
68927   68967   68975

Class A5 4-6-2T
69800   69805   69809   69812   69825

Class WD 2-8-0
90002   90064   90130   90235   90476
90005   90073   90146   90288   90496
90024   90075   90154   90296   90519
90025   90084   90161   90303   90618
90037   90103   90166   90368   90629
90038   90104   90185   90394   90634
90050   90115   90189   90432   90662
90052   90118   90202   90437   90703
90053   90120   90215   90473   90717

Class 9F 2-10-0
92186

Total 147

Allocations: 1965 (40E)

Class B1 4-6-0
61070   61248 Geoffrey Gibbs
61092   61264
61141   61281
61145   61285
61188   61299
61194   61302
61210   61361
61232   61390

Class 04 2-8-0
63639   63674   63707   63816   63873
63644   63675   63770   63819

Class WD 2-8-0
90002   90103   90413   90466   90629
90036   90104   90423   90492   90674
90037   90259   90432   90510   90703
90038   90316   90437   90545
90051   90393   90438   90606

Total 48

In January 1966 the depot found itself under the control of the London Midland Region which took over the Colwick area and injected some 57 LMR locos into the shed to replace the ER types.

At closure, in December 1966, the depot consisted solely of LMR engines, namely Stanier Classes 5 and 8 and BR Class 4. In view of the sparsity of steam power in the country as a whole at that time the remaining engines were transferred to 18 different depots on the LMR. A relatively small number were withdrawn but those surviving were not completely reallocated until three months later; thus, Colwick served into 1967 as a storage site.

As will be seen the shed was coded 16B under its brief LMR ownership.

A south-westerly view of Colwick depot in 1963. W. T. Stubbs

First of class No 61000 Springbok ('B1' 4-6-0) outside Colwick in 1961. This loco was allocated to Colwick between 1960 and its withdrawal in March 1962. K. Fairey

38B ANNESLEY

Pre-Grouping Origin: Great Central Railway
Gazetteer Ref: 41 E4
Closed: 1966
Shed-Codes: 38B (1949 to 1958)
16D (1958 to 1963)
16B (1963 to 1966)
Allocations: 1950 (38B)

Class B1 4-6-0
61063	61066	61209

Class K3 2-6-0
61943	61975	61977	61980
61974	61976	61979	

Classes O4 and O1 2-8-0*
63571	63639	63721	63795*	63863*
63578*	63646*	63722	63798	63867*
63579*	63662	63723	63799	63868*
63580	63674	63739	63803*	63869*
63589	63681	63742	63806*	63873
63594*	63687*	63743	63808*	63879*
63596	63689*	63746	63827	63893
63610*	63699	63748	63838	63901*
63614	63700	63752	63841	63912
63618	63706	63767	63853	
63635	63716	63792*	63858	

Class J11 0-6-0
64292	64318	64361	64431
64300	64354	64370	

Class J5 0-6-0
65494

Class C12 4-4-2T
67363	67387

Class J50 0-6-0T
68927	68929	68975	68976

Total 77

Allocations: 1959 (16D)

Class 4 2-6-4T
42333	42339	42361

Class 6P5F 2-6-0
42769	42784	42847	42872	42897

Class 3F 0-6-0T
47429	47458	47638

Class K3 2-6-0
61856	61975	61980

Class O1 2-8-0
63578	63689	63789	63817	63869
63579	63711	63792	63838	63886
63591	63740	63796	63854	63901
63610	63752	63806	63865	
63676	63777	63808	63867	

Class J11 0-6-0
64359	64375	64420	64439

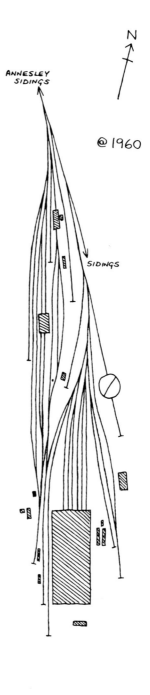

ANNESLEY
SIDINGS

@ 1960

N

SIDINGS

0   100   200   400
FEET

81

Class J39 0-6-0
64739	64747	64798	64955

Class 9F 2-10-0
92010	92067	92072	92081	92091
92011	92068	92073	92087	92092
92012	92069	92074	92088	92093
92013	92070	92075	92089	92095
92014	92071	92076	92090	92096

Total 70

Allocations: 1965 (16B)

Class 5MT 4-6-0
44665	44847	45215	45334	45406
44717	44848	45234	45335	45416
44835	44932	45301	45342	45450
44846	44984	45333	45346	

Class 8F 2-8-0
48037	48141	48168	48324	48661
48057	48142	48293	48363	
48079	48166	48304	48378	

Class 9F 2-10-0
92011	92033	92072	92088	92095
92013	92043	92073	92090	92096
92014	92067	92074	92091	92113
92030	92068	92075	92092	92132
92031	92069	92083	92093	92154
92032	92071	92087	92094	

Total 61

In 1958 the depot became London Midland property and began acquiring locos common to that region. At closure in January 1966 the few remaining engines mostly went to Derby and the 16B code was taken up by Colwick shed. The shed buildings were demolished in the same year.

A superb elevated view of the general layout at Annesley in 1937. W. Potter

Annesley in 1957 depicting BR '9F' 2-10-0s rubbing shoulders with ER types. The depot began acquiring the '9Fs' in this year. W. Potter

82

38C LEICESTER

Pre-Grouping Origin: Great Central Railway
Gazetteer Ref: 16 F3
Closed: 1964
Shed-Codes: 38C (1949 to 1958)
15E (1958 to 1963)
15D (1963 to 1964)
Allocations: 1950 (38C)

Class A3 4-6-2
60048 *Doncaster*
60049 *Galtee More*
60052 *Prince Palatine*
60054 *Prince of Wales*
60102 *Sir Frederick Banbury*
60103 *Flying Scotsman*
60104 *Solario*
60107 *Royal Lancer*

Class B1 4-6-0
61088	61108	61186	61298
61092	61141	61187	61299
61106	61185	61188	

Class J2 0-6-0
65015   65021

Class J5 0-6-0
65495

Class J50 0-6-0T
68981

Total 23

Allocations: 1959 (15E)

Class 3 2-6-2T
40165   40167   40182

Class 3F 0-6-0T
47203

Class V2 2-6-2
60831   60842   60863   60879   60911

Class B1 4-6-0
61008 *Kudu*	61269
61028 *Umseke*	61298
61063	61369
61085	61376
61106	61380
61137	61381
61201	

Class J6 0-6-0
64256

Total: 23

Leicester GCR was transferred to the London Midland Region in 1958 and closed as 15D in July 1964. The engines and men were re-allocated to Annesley 16B which itself had been an ER depot up to the 1958 regional boundary changes.

The other ER shed at Leicester was the ex-GNR three lane which, until closure in June 1955, served as a sub-shed to Leicester GCR. The engines were supplied by 38A Colwick from 1950 but the depot remained a sub to 38C as the latter continued to provide the crews. Leicester GNR was also known as 'Belgrave Road'.

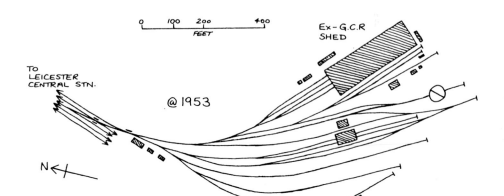

Looking south-east to Leicester shed in 1959 with two of its 'B1s' on display, Nos 61269 and 61063.
K. Fairey

A view of the side of Leicester depot on the same day showing the Tool Van, an unidentified 'B1' 4-6-0 and the sheer legs. K. Fairey

38D STAVELEY

Pre-Grouping Origin: Great Central Railway
Gazetteer Ref: 41 B3
Closed: 1965
Shed-Codes: 38D (1949 to 1958)
41H (1958 to 1965)
Allocations: 1950 (38D)

Class O4 2-8-0
63613	63702	63749
63694	63720	63859

Class J11 0-6-0
64317	64345	64386	64428	64444
64331	64384	64396	64433

Class J66 0-6-0T
68371	68379	68382

Class N5 0-6-2T
69279	69295	69351
69292	69301	69363

Class WD 2-8-0
90115	90276	90394	90418	90606
90269	90299	90403	90526	90634

Total 34

Allocations: 1959 (41H)

Class D11 4-4-0
62663 *Prince Albert*

Class O4 2-8-0
63648	63720	63772	63827	63884
63702	63735	63787	63845	63899
63705	63749	63801	63847	
63706	63762	63804	63877	

Class J11 0-6-0
64292	64336	64396	64444
64313	64384	64433	

Class J69 0-6-0T
68591

Class N5 0-6-2T
69263   69309

Class WD 2-8-0
90007	90085	90276	90418
90055	90087	90391	90502

Total 37

Allocations: 1965 (41H)

Classes O1 and O4* 2-8-0
63589	63630	63701*	63768	63879
63590	63646	63706*	63863	63913*
63612*	63650	63725	63868	

Class WD 2-8-0
90069	90227	90266	90401
90121	90258	90301	90719

Total 22

In 1952 the once twelve road installation was rebuilt to a five road structure and as one of the lanes was used for repair this meant that a good deal of the allocation was stabled in the open. The depot's closure in 1965 was a result of the withdrawal of freight services over the Great Central line. The engines were then transferred to Langwith Junction and the ex-LMR shed at Barrow Hill, Staveley. This latter depot of Midland origin was put under Eastern Region control in 1958 and was issued with the code 41E.

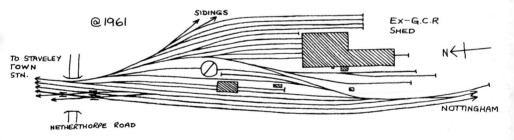

85

An overall view of Staveley shed in 1957 with
Class O4 locos dominating the metals. N. E. Preedy

Staveley Central in 1954 from a different angle
showing Classes J11 and O4 at rest outside.
N. E. Preedy

38E WOODFORD HALSE

Pre-Grouping Origin: Great Central Railway
Gazetteer Ref: 10 B4
Closed: 1965
Shed-Codes: 38E (1949 to 1958)
2G (1958)
2F (1958 to 1963)
1G (1963 to 1965)
Allocations: 1950 (38E)

Class V2 2-6-2
60815	60818	60826	60831	60845
60817	60820	60830	60832	60853

Class B17 4-6-0
61650 *Grimsby Town*	61664 *Liverpool*
61651 *Derby County*	61667 *Bradford*

Class J11 0-6-0
64324	64330	64369	64388	64408
64327	64364	64375	64390	64438

Class J39 0-6-0
64798
64838

Class L3 2-6-4T
69050   69069

Class N5 0-6-2T
69263	69269	69286	69310	69360

Class N2 0-6-2T
69560

Class WD 2-8-0
90033	90051	90137	90365	90509
90039	90065	90185	90486	90516
90040	90080	90218	90504	90520
90046	90095	90263	90507	90638

Total 54

Allocations: 1959 (2F)

Class 4 2-6-0
43063   43106

Class 3F 0-6-0
43330   43389   43394

Class V2 2-6-2
60815   60890   60915

Class B1 4-6-0
61078	61186	61192	61271	61368

Class K3 2-6-0
61804	61824	61841	61843
61809	61838	61842	61853

Class J10 0-6-0
65158

Class L1 2-6-4T
67740   67771   67789

Class WD 2-8-0
90033	90095	90365	90504	90672
90040	90137	90403	90507	90697
90046	90218	90433	90516	
90065	90237	90448	90520	
90066	90299	90474	90574	
90080	90346	90486	90638	

Total 51

Allocations: 1965 (IG)

Class 4MT 2-6-4T
42082   42103

Class 5MT 4-6-0
44762   44763   44764   44814

Class 8F 2-8-0
48002	48011	48088	48385
48005	48061	48121	48517
48010	48081	48336	48527

Total 18

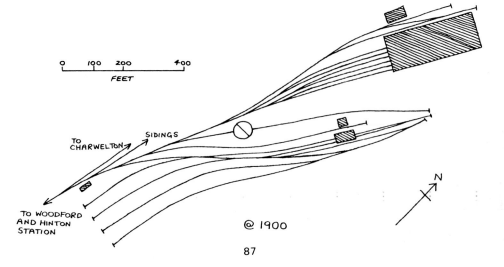

SIDINGS

TO
CHARWELTON

TO WOODFORD
AND HINTON
STATION

0   100   200   400
FEET

N

@ 1900

Woodford Halse found itself within the London Midland Region in 1958 taking up the code 2G. Within a few months the code was changed to 2F and remained so until 1963 when the depot received its final identity 1G. Closing in June 1965, the majority of its allocation was transferred to 1A Willesden.

Looking north to Woodford Halse shed in 1957, a year before its transfer to the LMR. W. Potter

Two Class 9Fs and a 'B1' outside Woodford Halse in 1960 whilst under LMR control (2F). K. Fairey

39A GORTON

Pre-Grouping Origin: Great Central Railway
Gazetteer Ref: 45 A3
Closed: 1965
Shed-Codes: 39A (1949 to 1958)
9H (1958)
9G (1958 to 1965)
Allocations: 1950 (39A)

Class B1 4-6-0

61114	61157	61160	61182	61225
61155	61158	61161	61184	61228
61156	61159	61162	61223	

Class K3 2-6-0

61808	61832	61856	61896	61914
61809	61839	61865	61908	61919
61828	61848	61870	61910	61950
61829	61852	61877	61913	61956

Classes O4 and O1* 2-8-0

63575	63638	63711*	63794	63876
63582	63641	63713	63796*	63880
63590*	63650*	63719	63805	63886*
63591*	63652*	63725*	63817*	63887*
63592*	63663*	63768*	63839	63890*
63598	63670*	63773*	63848	63891
63600	63678*	63777*	63854*	63895
63619*	63686	63780*	63862	63899
63630*	63695	63784*	63864	63915
63631	63705	63786*	63865*	
63633	63708	63789*	63872*	

Class J11 0-6-0

64294	64326	64357	64401	64437
64298	64332	64363	64409	64440
64311	64333	64368	64415	64450
64316	64342	64382	64434	
64322	64346	64383	64435	

Class J39 0-6-0

64712	64740	64744	64810	64972
64714	64741	64745	64824	
64717	64742	64748	64879	
64718	64743	64755	64962	

Class C13 4-4-2T

67401	67408	67417	67424	67437
67402	67410	67419	67425	67438
67403	67412	67421	67426	67439
67405	67415	67422	67427	
67407	67416	67423	67431	

Class J94 0-6-0ST

68012	68067	68071	68079

Class Y3 0-4-0T

68169

Class J71 0-6-0T

69250	69270	69299	69308
69260	69296	69307	

Class J88 0-6-0T

69333	69338	69347	69353

Total 166

Allocations: 1959 (9G)

Class 2 2-6-2T
41321

Class 1F 0-6-0T
41702

Class 4 2-6-4T

42328	42374	42429	42560

Class 3F 0-6-0

43187	43457	43638	43773
43207	43630	43763	

Class 4F 0-6-0

44025	44078	44114

Class 2F 0-6-0ST

51319	51484

Class B1 4-6-0

61161	61265

Class K3 2-6-0

61832	61865	61910	61913

Class O4 2-8-0

63573	63631	63709	63766	63862
63575	63641	63713	63767	63895
63582	63649	63716	63775	63915
63598	63681	63719	63794	
63600	63686	63721	63805	
63603	63700	63743	63848	

Class J11 0-6-0

64288	64310	64357	64389	64435
64294	64311	64363	64405	64437
64297	64331	64368	64418	64440
64298	64337	64382	64428	
64304	64341	64383	64434	

Class J39 0-6-0

64717	64740	64745	64824
64718	64742	64748	64875
64727	64743	64753	64930
64738	64744	64809	

Classes C13* and C14 4-4-2T

67417*	67450

Class L1 2-6-4T

67743	67751	67781	67796
67747	67756	67782	67798
67748	67762	67795	

Class J94 0-6-0ST

68012	68064	68068	68079

Class N5 0-6-2T

69307	69360

Class A5 4-6-2T

69801	69806	69813	69817	69823

Total 113

Allocations: 1965 (9G)

Class 4MT 2-6-4T

42327	42334	42368	42369

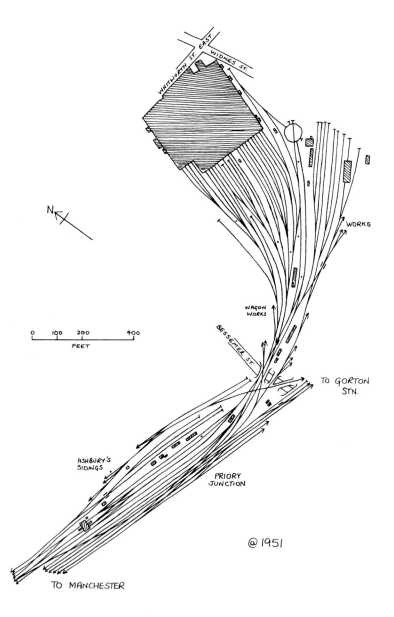

WHITWORTH ST. EAST

WIDNES ST.

N

0 100 200 400
FEET

WORKS

WAGON WORKS

BESSEMER ST.

TO GORTON STN.

ASHBURY'S SIDINGS

PRIORY JUNCTION

@ 1951

TO MANCHESTER

Class 5MT 2-6-0				
42700	42812	42844	42904	42940
42712	42819	42878	42905	
42715	42831	42901	42938	

Class 8F 2-8-0			
48176	48355	48515	48701
48178	48401	48543	48748
48322	48490	48557	

Class 5MT 2-6-0				
42945	42951	42964	42975	42981
42947	42955	42967	42978	42982
42950	42958	42974	42980	

Class 2MT 2-6-0		
78007	78012	78023
78011	78014	78062

Total 48

This principal ex-GCR depot was near to the large Locomotive works at Gorton and alongside the Wagon Works. In 1958 the shed became London Midland Region controlled and at closure in June 1965 the bulk of its engines were moved to other Manchester depots; 9B Stockport, 9D Newton Heath, 9E Trafford Park and 9H Heaton Mersey.

An overall view of the approaches to Gorton in 1936. W. Potter

Looking east from the top of the depot's coaling plant in the same year. Gorton Works is visible in the distance whilst the foreground portrays the ash plant and Priory Junction. As will be seen in the diagram, the coal and ash facilities were some distance from the shed building. W. Potter

91

39B SHEFFIELD DARNALL

Pre-Grouping Origin: Great Central Railway
Gazetteer Ref: 42 G2
Closed: 1963
Shed-Codes: 39B (1949 to 1955)
41A (1955 to 1963)
Allocations: 1950 (39B)

Class B1 4-6-0

61145	61153	61181	61313	61317
61150	61154	61183	61314	61327
61151	61169	61311	61315	
61152	61179	61312	61316	

Class O4 2-8-0

63574	63622	63710	63771	63846
63581	63629	63714	63783	63850
63583	63661	63733	63790	63860
63604	63675	63734	63797	63882
63605	63680	63737	63821	63888
63609	63685	63766	63822	63889

Class J11 0-6-0

64291	64373	64419	64445
64336	64387	64441	64447
64360	64412	64443	

Class J39 0-6-0

64746	64808	64878	64903	64969
64753	64809	64890	64960	64973

@ 1955

To SHEFFIELD

ROAD

To DARNALL STATION

N

0   100   200   400

FEET

Class C13 4-4-2T

67404	67406

Class Y3 0-4-0T

68176	68184

Class J50 0-6-0T

68928	68983	68990

Class J72 0-6-0T

68015

Class N4 0-6-2T

69225	69230	69234	69240	69246
69227	69231	69235	69242	
69228	69232	69236	69244	
69229	69233	69239	69245	

Total 94

Allocations: 1959 (41A)

Class B1 4-6-0
61033 *Dibatag*

61041	61083	61152	61181	61327
61044	61105	61153	61183	61334
61047	61138	61154	61313	
61050	61150	61162	61315	
61051	61151	61169	61316	

Class K2 2-6-0

61728	61747	61760	61761

Class K3 2-6-0

61816	61907	61943
61825	61938	61967

Class D11 4-4-0
62660 *Butler-Henderson*
62661 *Gerard Powys Dewhurst*
62662 *Prince of Wales*
62664 *Princess Mary*
62665 *Mons*
62666 *Zeebrugge*
62667 *Somme*
62668 *Jutland*
62669 *Ypres*
62670 *Marne*

Class 04 2-8-0

63574	63640	63710	63783	63882
63583	63645	63733	63821	63888
63599	63658	63734	63822	63889
63604	63661	63737	63846	
63609	63680	63742	63850	
63621	63685	63748	63852	
63624	63695	63771	63881	

Class J11 0-6-0

64329	64387	64419	64443	64447
64373	64394	64441	64445	

Class J39 0-6-0

64702	64736	64804	64808
64719	64746	64807	64878

Class N5 0-6-2T

69258	69294	69314
69290	69296	69361

Total 97

Darnall lost its steam allocation in June 1963 and although it is known that the depot stored and turned visiting locos after this date, it can reasonably be assumed that the shed closed to all steam later the same year. The depots at 41D Canklow and 41F Mexborough took charge of the displaced Darnall stud.

In 1950 it will be seen that Darnall boasted all the surviving Class N4 locos. This class became extinct a few years later.

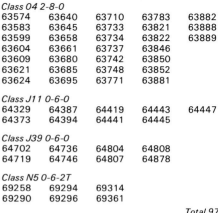

An easterly view of Sheffield Darnall shed in 1960 as taken from the nearby road overbridge. K. Fairey

Another view of the western end of Darnall, this time in 1952 as 39B. LGRP, courtesy David & Charles

40A LINCOLN

Pre-Grouping Origin: Great Northern Railway
Gazetteer Ref: 16 B1
Closed: 1964
Shed-Code: 40A (1949 to 1964)
Allocations: 1950

Class B1 4-6-0

61112	61279	61281	61364
61269	61280	61329	61405

Class K3 2-6-0

61807	61859	61925	61960	61966
61822	61894	61944	61964	61982

Class C4 4-4-2T

62908	62918

Class J11 0-6-0

64303	64350	64359	64371
64315	64351	64365	64430

Class J39 0-6-0

64702	64728	64738	64883	64937
64715	64730	64789	64886	64971
64722	64734	64804	64887	
64725	64736	64881	64904	

Class C12 4-4-2T

67389

Class J66 0-6-0T

68376	68385

Classes J67* and J69 0-6-0T

68529*	68553	68587	68610*
68537	68558	68599	68618

Class N5 0-6-2T

69253	69275	69287	69311

Class A5 4-6-2T

69804	69813	69820

Total 64

Allocations: 1959

Class 1P 0-4-4T

58065

Class B1 4-6-0

61009 *Hartebeeste*		61248 *Geoffrey Gibbs*
61026 *Ourebi*		61258
61202		61405

Class K3 2-6-0

61802	61828	61889	61944
61806	61848	61894	61960
61807	61859	61919	

Class J6 0-6-0

64207	64219	64278

Class J11 0-6-0

64318	64371	64430

Class J39 0-6-0

64726	64751	64889	64937	64961
64734	64755	64890	64959	64966
64741	64881	64896	64960	64984

Class L1 2-6-4T

67769

Class J69 0-6-0T

68501	68528	68560	68599
68510	68543	68581	

Class A5 4-6-2T

69803	69808	69820	69821

Total 51

Scrutiny of the 1959 allocation will show that the ex-Midland Rly tank No 58065 was part of the depot's stud in that year. It was transferred with its sister engine 58085 from 36E Retford in January 1959 and both continued taking turns on the Southwell Branch from Lincoln. 58085 does not appear in the above listing as it was withdrawn by the date to which the list refers (April 1959).

When the shed closed in January 1964, the few remaining locos went to 36E Retford.

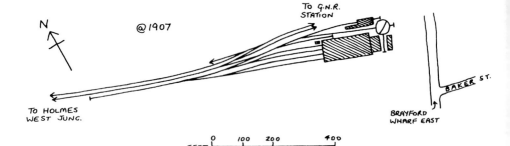

@ 1907

N

To G.N.R. STATION

BAKER ST.

To HOLMES WEST JUNC.

BRAYFORD WHARF EAST

FEET 0 100 200 400

A 1951 view of Lincoln yard, apparently on the occasion of a society visit. N. E. Preedy

Classes K3 2-6-0 and J39 0-6-0 Nos 61828 and 64728 (both 40A) outside the rebuilt depot at Lincoln in 1958. British Rail

40B IMMINGHAM

Pre-Grouping Origin: Great Central Railway
Gazetteer Ref: 22 E2
Closed: 1966
Shed-Code: 40B (1949 to 1966)
Allocations: 1950

Class B1 4-6-0

61079	61191	61284	61365	61408
61082	61195	61318	61366	61409
61142	61202	61325	61406	
61190	61204	61328	61407	

Class K2 2-6-0

61720	61724	61728
61722	61727	61733

Class K3 2-6-0

61800	61806	61836	61842	61905
61802	61825	61837	61845	61912
61803	61827	61838	61891	61963

Class D11 4-4-0
62660 Butler-Henderson
62661 Gerard Powys Dewhurst
62662 Prince of Wales
62664 Princess Mary
62666 Zeebrugge
62667 Somme
62668 Jutland
62669 Ypres

Class C4 4-4-2

62909	62919

Class O4 2-8-0

63586	63621	63657	63738	63878
63593	63624	63692	63802	
63607	63647	63693	63819	
63616	63651	63698	63836	

Class J11 0-6-0

64284	64312	64325	64411
64305	64314	64355	64439
64307	64323	64372	64446

Class J94 0-6-0ST

68009	68026	68068	68074	68080
68013	68028	68069	68075	
68018	68030	68070	68076	
68020	68033	68072	68077	
68022	68034	68073	68078	

Class Y3 0-4-0T

68162	68179

Class J63 0-6-0T

68204	68206	68208	68210
68205	68207	68209	

Class N5 0-6-2T

69305	69309	69322

Class A5 4-6-2T
69800

Class WD 2-8-0

90032	90133	90456	90646
90075	90162	90460	90647

Total 120

N

@ 1964

FEET
0   100   200   400

THE SHED WAS SITED NEAR TO THE SOUTH-WEST PART
OF IMMINGHAM DOCKS AND WAS NOT VERY EASY TO FIND.
10 METRE NATIONAL GRID REF. Nº-: TA19831513.

DOCKS   SIDINGS

Allocations: 1959

Class B1 4-6-0

61079	61143	61190	61328	61406
61082	61144	61195	61366	61408
61098	61159	61284	61374	61409
61130	61168	61318	61379 *Mayflower*	
61142	61175	61325	61390	

Class K2 2-6-0

61730	61745	61763	61767	61773
61740	61756	61766	61771	61778

Class K3 2-6-0

61866	61905	61950	61966
61891	61912	61956	

Class O4 2-8-0

63615	63651	63738	63819	63878
63616	63692	63750	63837	63900
63644	63708	63759	63860	

Class J11 0-6-0

64284	64325	64386
64305	64355	64446

Class J94 0-6-0ST

68009	68018	68070	68074	68078

Class A5 4-6-2T

69829

Class WD 2-8-0

90003	90145	90280	90443	90648
90029	90175	90285	90460	90674
90035	90221	90294	90471	
90036	90224	90383	90510	
90131	90263	90393	90583	

Class 9F 2-10-0

92039	92194	92196
92193	92195	92202

Total 94

Allocations: 1965

Class B1 4-6-0

61003 *Gazelle*	61223
61026 *Ourebi*	61250 *A. Harold Bibby*
61042	61365
61089	61370
61098	61389
61168	61406
61195	

Class WD 2-8-0

90029	90075	90242	90443	90662
90035	90142	90294	90660	

Class 9F 2-10-0

92035	92193	92194	92197	92202

Total 27

The south-east end of Immingham shed in 1962 showing 'B1' and '9F' classes in between turns of duty. The extreme right illustrates a portion of the diesel accommodation. K. Fairey

In 1950 Immingham played host to all the 'J63' 0-6-0T class and, with the exception of No 68209 from December 1951, continued to do so until their eventual demise in 1957.

Not closing to steam until February 1966, the shed became one of the last depots on the Eastern Region to boast a steam allocation. At closure the remaining locos went to 36A Doncaster to take part in the last few months of the region's steam operation. (See 36A.)

An overall view of Immingham showing the other end of the through road building. M. S. Houlgrave

40C LOUTH

Pre-Grouping Origin: Great Northern Railway
Gazetteer Ref: 22 G2
Closed: 1956
Shed-Code: 40C (1949 to 1956)
Allocations: 1950

Class D3 4-4-0
62132

Class J11 0-6-0
64320   64328

Class C12 4-4-2T
67352   67379   67383   67398
67364   67381   67384

Class N5 0-6-2T
69306

Total 11

Closing in December 1956 as a result of dieselisation, the last three remaining locos (Nos 64320, 64328 and 67398) were moved to 40B Immingham.

The north end of Louth in the early 1950s with Class C12 4-4-2T No 67384 (40C) in the foreground.
B. Yale

Class C12 No 4525 standing outside the south entrance of Louth shed in 1946. At nationalisation this engine became BR No 67379 and remained in service at Louth until late 1955 when it was transferred to 35C Peterborough Spital Bridge.
H. C. Casserley

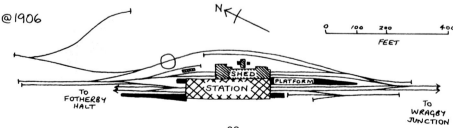

40D TUXFORD

Pre-Grouping Origin: Great Central Railway
Gazetteer Ref: 16 B2
Closed: 1959
Shed-Codes: 40D (1949 to 1958)
41K (1958 to 1959)
Allocations: 1950 (40D)

Class 04 2-8-0

63570	63634	63852	63885
63588	63691	63861	

Class J11 0-6-0

64286	64299	64344	64392
64293	64337	64353	64424

Total 15

Upon closure in February 1959, the engines and men transferred to Langwith Junction 41J.

Looking north-east to Tuxford depot in 1956 showing two-thirds of the roof missing. This portion was the original two lane structure, the south-easterly lane being covered at a later date.   K. Fairey

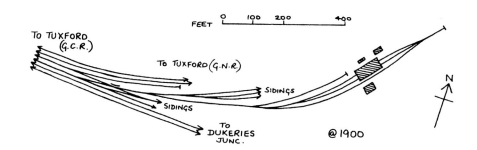

Tuxford shed in 1953 with (left to right) Class 04s Nos 63885, 63852 and 'J11' No 64344 (all 40D).
Photomatic

40E LANGWITH JUNCTION

Pre-Grouping Origin: Great Central Railway
Gazetteer Ref: 41 C4
Closed: 1966
Shed-Codes: 40E (1949 to 1958)
41J (1958 to 1966)
Allocations: 1950 (40E)

Class O4 2-8-0

63577	63656	63707	63758	63837
63585	63658	63709	63759	63840
63597	63665	63715	63765	63842
63615	63666	63717	63776	63870
63625	63677	63724	63800	63884
63632	63679	63741	63807	63900
63644	63683	63750	63809	63902
63648	63703	63757	63833	

Class J11 0-6-0

64281	64310	64378	64414	64427
64289	64321	64379	64418	
64297	64358	64389	64426	

Class N5 0-6-2T

69284	69319	69323	69327

Class A5 4-6-2T

69812	69815	69818

Class Q1 0-8-0T

69928	69929

Total 61

Allocations: 1959 (41J)

Class O4 2-8-0

63577	63636	63703	63758	63842
63597	63643	63707	63765	63853
63607	63664	63715	63776	63861
63622	63665	63717	63800	63870
63632	63679	63722	63829	63893
63634	63683	63732	63833	63902
63635	63691	63739	63840	63912

Class J11 0-6-0

64314	64324	64346	64362	64427
64316	64332	64352	64364	
64317	64333	64354	64379	

Class J94 0-6-0ST

68026	68080

Class J69 0-6-0T

68554

Class N5 0-6-2T

69286	69299

Class WD 2-8-0

90043	90259	90411	90492	90594
90051	90275	90431	90545	90657
90088	90287	90438	90554	
90162	90302	90449	90577	

Total 71

Allocations: 1965 (41J)

Class O4 2-8-0

63679	63697	63739	63843	63882
63691	63732	63828	63850	63893

Class WD 2-8-0

90043	90271	90292	90418
90088	90275	90398	90449

Class 9F 2-10-0

92040	92141	92146	92178	92189
92041	92144	92148	92179	92191
92042	92145	92149	92182	92195

Total 33

At closure in February 1966, the depot's last three locos (Nos 61050, 61051 and 61315) were transferred to departmental stock for use as stationary boilers using numbers 30/1/2 respectively. A noteworthy point is that Langwith played host to the last serving ex-GCR type, namely No 63612 withdrawn in November 1965.

@ 1959

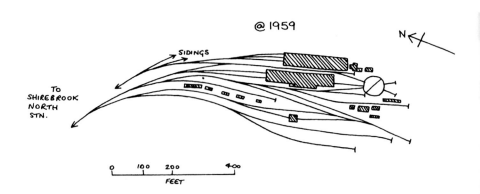

100

A southerly view of Langwith in 1954. The presence of groups of adult spotters would suggest that the depot was being visited by a railway society.
Photomatic

Looking south-east to the two lane building at Langwith in 1957 with Classes K1 No 62067 (31B) and J11 No 64293 (40E) nearest the camera.
W. Potter

40F BOSTON

Pre-Grouping Origin: Great Northern Railway
Gazetteer Ref: 17 C3
Closed: 1964
Shed-Code: 40F (1949 to 1964)
Allocations: 1950

Class K2 2-6-0

61725	61744	61755	61760	61770
61731	61750	61756	61762	

Class D2 4-4-0
62154   62181

Class C4 4-4-2T
62900   62901

Class J3 0-6-0
64115   64132   64137

Class J6 0-6-0

64180	64196	64204	64242	64248
64181	64198	64210	64244	64276
64190	64201	64229	64247	

Class J2 0-6-0
65016   65017   65020

Class C12 4-4-2T
67350

Class Y3 0-4-0T
68166S   68171

Class J69 0-6-0T
68528   68543   68560   68581

Class J68 0-6-0T
68655   68657   68658   68659

Class N5 0-6-2T
69256   69261   69280

Class A5 4-6-2T
69808   69819

Total 49

Allocations: 1959

Class 4 2-6-0

43058	43065	43091	43108	43147
43059	43066	43092	43109	43157
43060	43068	43093	43110	43159
43061	43080	43095	43111	
43062	43083	43104	43142	
43064	43085	43107	43143	

Class K2 2-6-0

61731	61743	61750	61762
61742	61748	61751	

Class J6 0-6-0

64171	64190	64229	64250
64172	64191	64231	64260
64180	64214	64247	

Class J39 0-6-0
64728   64729   64823

Class J69 0-6-0T
68557   68570   68602

T

At steam closure in January 1964, the entire allocation consisting of Ivatt Class 4s were transferred to New England and Colwick.

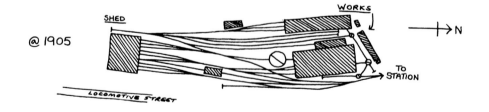

@ 1905

SHED

WORKS

→N

TO STATION

LOCOMOTIVE STREET

FEET 0 100 200 400

This 1961 view of Boston shows the main nine road building as seen from the North. At this time the depot possessed 23 Class 4 2-6-0s and at least five can be seen here.   K. Fairey

This 1958 view of Boston shows the sidings and repair shed which faced the main building.   B. Hilton

41A SHEFFIELD DARNALL

(See 39B Sheffield Darnall — This volume.)

41B SHEFFIELD GRIMESTHORPE
41C MILLHOUSES
41D CANKLOW
41E STAVELEY MIDLAND

Refer to:
19A Sheffield Grimesthorpe
19B Millhouses
19C Canklow
18D Staveley Midland

within the LMR volume

(All four depots were of Midland Railway origin. They did not transfer to the Eastern Region until 1958 and have been catered for in the LMR book.)

41F MEXBOROUGH

(See 36B Mexborough — This volume.)

41G BARNSLEY

(See 36D Barnsley — This volume.)

41H STAVELEY CENTRAL

(See 38D Staveley Central — This volume.)

41J LANGWITH JUNCTION

(See 40E Langwith Junction — This volume.)

41K TUXFORD

(See 40D Tuxford — This volume.)

LIST OF SHED CODES

The following list sets out every shed-code that existed for steam Motive Power Depots under the Eastern Region from 1949 to 1966 along with each venue and its length of occupancy.

30A	Stratford	1949-62
30B	Hertford East	1949-60
30C	Bishops Stortford	1949-59
30D	Southend Victoria	1949-57
30E	Colchester	1949-59
30F	Parkeston	1949-61
31A	Cambridge	1949-62
31B	March	1949-63
31C	Kings Lynn	1949-59
31D	South Lynn	1949-59
31E	Bury St Edmunds	1949-59
31F	Peterborough Spital Bridge	1958-60
32A	Norwich	1949-62
32B	Ipswich	1949-59
32C	Lowestoft	1949-60
32D	Yarmouth South Town	1949-59
32E	Yarmouth Vauxhall	1949-59
32F	Yarmouth Beach	1949-59
32G	Melton Constable	1949-59
33A	Plaistow	1949-59
33B	Tilbury	1949-62
33C	Shoeburyness	1949-62
34A	Kings Cross	1949-63
34B	Hornsey	1949-61
34C	Hatfield	1949-61
34D	Hitchin	1949-61
34E	Neasden	1949-58
	New England	1958-65
34F	Grantham	1958-63
35A	New England	1949-58
35B	Grantham	1949-58
35C	Peterborough Spital Bridge	1950-58
36A	Doncaster	1949-66
36B	Mexborough	1949-58
36C	Frodingham	1949-66
36D	Barnsley	1949-58
36E	Retford	1949-65
37A	Ardsley	1949-56
37B	Copley Hill	1949-56
37C	Bradford Hammerton St	1949-56
38A	Colwick	1949-58
38B	Annesley	1949-58
38C	Leicester Central	1949-58
38D	Staveley Central	1949-58
38E	Woodford Halse	1949-58
39A	Gorton	1949-58
39B	Sheffield Darnall	1949-55
40A	Lincoln	1949-64
40B	Immingham	1949-66

40C	Louth 1949-56
40D	Tuxford 1949-58
40E	Langwith Junction 1949-58
	Colwick 1958-66
40F	Boston 1949-64

41A	Sheffield Darnall 1955-63
41B	Sheffield Grimesthorpe 1958-61
41C	Millhouses 1958-62
41D	Canklow 1958-65
41E	Staveley Midland 1958-65
41F	Mexborough 1958-64
41G	Barnsley 1958-60
41H	Staveley Central 1958-65
41J	Langwith Junction 1958-66
41K	Tuxford 1958-59

Before groups 30A to 40F were finally chosen, consideration was given to the undermentioned codes for the Western Section of the Eastern Region. It will be seen that Wrexham Rhosddu and Bidston would have become 39C and 39D respectively had they not been transferred to the LMR in 1949.

40ABCDE   Kings Cross, Hornsey, Hatfield, Hitchin, Neasden
41AB   New England, Grantham
42ABCDE   Doncaster, Mexborough, Frodingham, Barnsley, Retford
43ABC   Ardsley, Copley Hill, Bradford Hammerton Street
44ABCDE   Colwick, Annesley, Leicester Central, Staveley Central, Woodford Halse
45ABCD   Gorton, Sheffield Darnall, Wrexham Rhosddu, Bidston
46ABCDEF   Lincoln, Immingham, Louth, Tuxford, Langwith Junction, Boston

Shedplates

Made of cast-iron and measuring $7\frac{1}{4}'' \times 4\frac{1}{2}''$, shed plates were fitted to every BR steam locomotive on the engine's smokebox door. The code thereon related to the home depot and their use was a boon to railway staff and enthusiasts alike. As would be expected, when a locomotive transferred to another shed its plate was changed but towards the end of steam traction when closures and movements abounded many engines simply had a painted code in place of a plate.

105

Looking south from the Queens Road level crossing near to 36D Barnsley, (See 36D plan). The sidings shown are either side of the main line and illustrate the need for space which was a factor of many small depots with a proportionately large allocation. Photograph taken in 1957.   W. Potter

Another view of Retford GCR, this time in 1951 showing the modus operandi for removal of ash from the pits and lineside which existed at that time. Many of the larger depots had ash-plants constructed which considerably streamlined this operation but a surprising number of sheds were forced to use the illustrated method until closure in the 1960s. W. Potter

Class 04 2-8-0 No 63702 (36E) under the sheer-legs at Retford GCR in 1963. These steel tripods were fairly common on the Eastern Region and were invaluable for a host of repairs and functions. K. Fairey

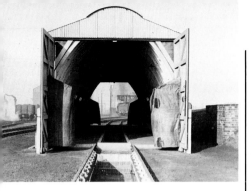

A north-westerley view through the illuminated inspection pit at Peterborough New England (35A) soon after construction in LNER days. Installations such as this were only to be found at main sheds, but notwithstanding this, their existence in the form illustrated was quite rare. British Rail

The demolition of a coaling plant at a depot almost always necessitated the use of explosives because of their reinforced construction and height. Portrayed here is the demise of the 70ft high Kings Cross coaler in April 1964. British Rail

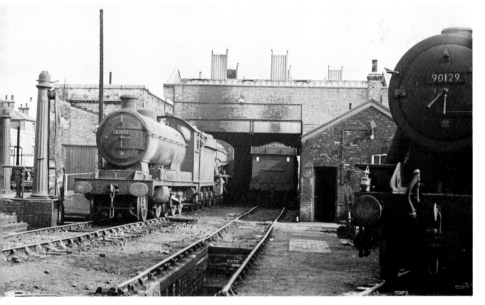

Before and after. Two views of Retford GCR taken in 1963 and 1965 from an identical vantage point. The 'before' photograph shows Class 04 2-8-0 No 63651 (36E) on the left with WD 2-8-0 No 90129 (40B) nearest the camera. The site was cleared to make way for BR's modernisation programme (See 36E). Both: J. S. Hancock

The practice of visiting sheds on a Sunday was a popular event as most of the allocated locos could be found 'on shed'. This view of Immingham on such a day in 1963 shows left to right: (All 40B unless stated) Nos 92202, 63706 (41H), 92197, 61056, 92196, 61365, 61026, 90221, 90180, 70037, 90225 (36A), 61003.   A. W. Martin

Looking north to the 'wash-out' shed at March 31B in 1951 with 'D16', 'J15' and 'K3' examples facing the camera. The provision of a building for this function was a comparative luxury as most sheds had to carry out this task amid cramped stabling conditions.   W. Potter

Ex LTSR '69' class 0-6-2T No 41990 (33C) at Plaistow 33A in 1952. The greater majority of engines inherited from the smaller pre-grouping companies were withdrawn in the 1950s being replaced by the influx of BR standard designs. Sadly, a great many once-numerous classes were rendered extinct by the cutter's torch thus leaving only photographic and documented evidence of their existence.   K. Fairey

A 1958 view of the north end of Doncaster 36A showing the twin road coaling plant. Facing left to right are O2 2-8-0 No 63963 (36A), K3 2-6-0 No 61826 (31B) and B1 4-6-0 No 61036 Ralph Assheton (36A).   W. Potter

Looking east across Gorton Yard 39A in 1938 with an '04' and a variety of tank classes to the fore. W. Potter

WD class 2-8-0 No 90634, a Colwick engine, stands outside Gorton shed in 1958. This type of engine was not normally seen in such a clean condition and it is quite likely that the loco had received a recent overhaul.   A. G. Ellis

Sheffield Darnall boasted two 'Royal Scot' class engines amongst its allocation in 1962 and one of them is seen here inside the depot in July of that year, No 46151 The Royal Horse Guardsman. The other loco was No 46164 The Artists' Rifleman. They were not at Darnall very long as both were withdrawn in December 1962.   M. S. Eggenton

Woodford Halse depot in October 1963 in its final guise as 1G within the London Midland Region. Note that the loco being watered is a visiting '22xx' class 0-6-0 No 2246 (85A Worcester) which will have worked in with a freight turn.   J. R. P. Hunt

Hornsey shed (34B) a few years after the grouping in 1925.   Real Photos

Kings Cross (34A) in Great Northern days. Note the modern hydraulic lifting gear on the right compared with the earlier twin road hand operated structure in front of the running shed. A GNR Atlantic type can be seen underneath the hydraulic apparatus.
Ian Allan Library

Woodford Halse (38E) in Great Central days. Note the clock between the centre lanes, this was a feature of many GCR sheds notably 34E Neasden and 38C Leicester. Ian Allan Library

A group of shed-plates from the Author's collection. Note the contrasting styles of lettering among the LMR groups and the comparative uniformity of the Eastern Region examples.

Index